RAZIYAHU HALEVEY

REFLECTIONS WITHIN THE MIRROR OF RADIANCE

Volume I: Instructions for Realizing the Mystical Mind

DRUKAMA
TREASURY™

First published by Drukama 2020

Prepublication copy

First edition

ISBN: 978-1-7359754-0-5

Editing by Ginger Marcus
Proofreading by Andrew Pleavin
Cover art by Teenuja Dahari
Illustration by Kevin Mangaroo

This book was professionally typeset on Reedsy.
Find out more at reedsy.com

To the future heroes who will
disseminate this teaching, illuminating many.

＊ ＊ ＊

To my teachers who taught me the basis
for realization, easing me into the pith for breakthrough.

＊ ＊ ＊

To my beloved mother Amayana who bestowed her wisdom, fed me knowledge,
and disciplined with understanding through enduring patience.

＊ ＊ ＊

Finally, to my Sati, the radiance within my reflection.

The Field of Dreams

+++

Untying knots of entanglements that
perceive independent origination;
the path of self-realization.

Seer and seen are hearer and heard; all rising
and falling phenomena within the field of
dreamy perception.

Beyond movement and stillness is the true
mind; changeless, illumined, and brilliant.

When the thread becomes fetterless, perception of interdependent origination seals the
uniquely penetrative supreme spontaneity.

~ Raziyahu

Contents

From the Editor   iii

Introduction   v

I   THEORY

 1 Approaching the Method   3
 2 The Intention Behind Realization   11
 3 Mysticism and the Intellect   16
 4 The Path of Authentic Realization   23
 5 Emptiness and Awareness   34
 6 Phenomena   39
 7 The Field of Perception   43
 8 Desire   49
 9 Delusion, Confusion, and Suffering   53
10 The Mental Aggregates   56
11 Elements, Channels, and Centers   58
12 The Right View   68
13 Adjusting Single-Pointed Focus   75
14 Mystical Union   78
15 Mystical Visions   81
16 The Practice Area   90
17 Physical Well-Being   96
18 Meditative Postures   98
19 Breathing Techniques   111

II PRACTICE

20	Preliminary Meditation	119
21	Energy Purification	123
22	Elemental Cultivation	126
23	Clarification of Branches	128
24	Preparing the Central Channel	130
25	Gift-Blessings Offering	132
26	Refining Space	136
27	Refining Fire	139
28	Refining Air	141
29	Preliminary View	143
30	Earth Arousal	149
31	Water Arousal	152
32	Fire Arousal	154
33	Bliss-Warmth	156
34	Air Arousal	159
35	Space Arousal	162
36	Clear Light Mystic Vision	164
37	Preliminary Dream Projection	169
38	Dark Light Mystic Vision	172
39	Dream and Deep Sleep View	176
40	Sealing Realization	180
41	Conclusion	184
Index		186
About the Author		192

From the Editor

The prepublication volume you hold in your hands marks the beginning; it provides a firm sense of what is to come, and contains the necessary instructions for you to start the method while awaiting the polished first edition.

If making use of this less refined version of the manual, be sure to seek clarification and instruction within the group at the Drukama Treasury, and inquire there to obtain the finalized text to replace this volume for ongoing study and application.

* * *

The care and dedication invested in the development of the first edition of this book may not be visible in the printed pages, but the significance of the work will be apparent to seekers navigating the deeper mysteries of the spiritual path. These teachings are part of a living practice system, and while future editions are expected to evolve and enhance aspects of the text, the core message and purpose will remain steady, as it has throughout history.

This singular ancient mystical path was split and concealed, and mysticism ultimately became associated with diverse and rich cultures. Plain terms have been employed to help bridge these teachings into modern American English in a way that is more digestible for a global audience almost wholly disconnected from its universal roots. Traditional terms included by the author are useful to help correlate the ideas. The authentic mystical path may appear to draw from various cultures, but it is more accurate to view it as a unified base for the range of widely accepted models.

Many revelations are set forth in this text, and they need not be adopted blindly; they are meant to be lived. I can attest that the author has no need for the reader to believe or accept his experiences and claims; he is inviting practitioners to inquire and discover the truth of the path firsthand, through the method. His own expertise is in the fullness and depth of the human experience, as well as in what lies beyond the normal limited spheres of perception. His words and intention will inspire and stir true seekers to greater heights of clarity, and ultimately toward liberation from the need to depend on outside sources for information about the reality we share.

The spiritual messages in this volume are also timely. Later editions can be made to improve overall readability; in this case, sharing the basis of the teachings with the people without delay was deemed far more important than meeting conventional publishing guidelines. The aspirants who have waited so patiently for these previously concealed instructions to be released in this format will understand and appreciate why the text has been delivered in this way, and this book is for those dedicated souls. They will carry the method forward, living the word, so that all can come to know its fruits in good time.

All the best to you on your path.

Introduction

First, let me apologize to you. I am a simple, uneducated man who for a portion of his life reigned as the king of unconscious egoists. Please bear with me as I try to elucidate one of life's most intense and misunderstood subjects: the mystical path of self-realization. Heaven help me.

I'll do the best I can, and if you are patient and merciful, you may find helpful ideas that might make your life experience more intense and enjoyable, connecting you to a profound radiant clarity that changes perception from one dissatisfying experience after another into a continuous, bountiful adventure.

The method presented here represents the knowledge of the path of self-realization that I used, as it was taught to me over a long period of time. I hope you uncover treasures here that help make the path much easier for you than it was for me.

* * *

When I was a child, my first teacher would only accept my questions after I had carefully and thoughtfully considered them. I had to form my questions without bias and in a way that helped not just me, but everyone around me. If a question was not posed with the right intention, it was ignored, or worse.

He would also remind me that most of my questions could be answered by contemplating them diligently beforehand. Of course, he was right. When I asked a question that I had not thought through, I would pay for it in the form of a tongue-lashing or by a response that confused and entangled me deeper into the question, forcing me to go back and investigate my thoughts more thoroughly. He was trying to teach me to be my own source of knowledge and wisdom, and that lesson was extremely valuable.

Through his lessons, I learned how to listen to people more effectively, and that listening helped me become more compassionate and force away my own biases, allowing people the right to be right and to express themselves openly, even if my inner ego-bias objected.

Belittling someone or arguing against their expressions is a kind of suppression, a kind of war against their freedoms. More patient, forgiving, thoughtful, and compassionate interaction is needed in the world now, more than ever, and this was my teacher's intention.

But to gain the ability to interact in this way, a thorough understanding of oneself, one's problem, and the inherent solution is required. One seeking to reveal the natural state of freedom and authentic expression need not create anything new. All that is required is to get things out of the way so that the pure essential nature can emerge in greater degrees of clarity and strength—the true expression of what one really was, is, and will always be.

Realization is not limited to selfish examination for reaching personal bliss and radiantly clear perception; it also brings about positive changes in the individual that influence the rest of humanity. It is not just another interesting exploration; it is a vital life experience. The illumination gained from the journey can bring about the inclusive and connected interactions that are so desperately needed today. It is incumbent on one to reveal the essential nature for one's own benefit and to benefit others. In my opinion, this journey should be offered to every young person around the globe.

However, many who attempt to teach this path have not attained its fruits. People misunderstand realization, and the so-called spiritual community has been flooded with "free" teachings that are not worth the price. While it is vital and healthy for people to seek the truth together and to share experiences and thoughts about the path, instruction regarding the authentic process of gradual and systematic penetration of the subconscious mind should come from someone who has already achieved it. One must fully understand what the path is, not just guess at how it is supposed to work using a confused and deluded mind. Many veteran seekers have come to me from other schools or traditions, asking for help, only to find their approach to the path was not realistic for breakthrough.

There are many ways to achieve the clear, stream-realized state; what is described here is the main method I was taught. Though no method is truly required for one to attain what already exists, there are a number of ways to reduce the habitual tendency noise concealing one's essential nature. This specific approach is an intense, powerful, and efficient system for achievement of that goal. Over the decades, I have yet to discover a more effective one, but that certainly does not mean they do not exist.

This system is presented in a way that I hope anyone at any level can understand. But my attempts to make the method easier to understand and accomplish do not make the journey itself any less potent. I am not suggesting that one should simply trust, heaven forbid, that this approach must be used. With any practical application, one must understand the reasons for doing it relative to short-term and long-term objectives. For this purpose, I have tried to detail the challenge of the subtle energy disturbances, how they influence the awareness, how to awaken awareness by subduing these disturbances to ultimately produce the revelation of emptiness, and how to unify the awareness with emptiness to achieve fully sealed realization.

I never had a desire to teach this process, but seeing the great demand for authentic and clear explanation without concealment or confusion, I felt the need to try to help. Of the countless books available on spirituality, mysticism, and the occult, very few have offered open and plain revelations of the typically concealed teachings I have tried to elucidate in this series.

I refused many public interviews over the years, and was content teaching in small groups that requested clarification. However, the landscape has recently changed, and there is now a massive cry for accurate instruction to overcome misunderstandings. I have spent more than 50 years watching this world mature, watching the people in it become more open to the investigation of the subtle dimensions. I made the decision to share what I know at this time, because it is imperative that people become wakeful before more damage and separation occurs on our planet. I hope this information can help, in some way, to bring people together through radiantly clear, compassionate, and luminous perception.

Since 2005, I have written a mountain of articles on the subject of mysticism, given thousands of private lectures, held retreats, provided initiations into the path, and helped many people begin to journey along what I consider to be the ultimate process of evolution. It is our mission's aim to now share these teachings openly so they can be demonstrated and elucidated by the school's expert lecturers, whose intention is to support each seeker. I hope that you will feel capable to carry that torch and help elucidate these teachings at some point as well.

This method of realization is not owned by anyone. The commentary is mine and the way I explain the concepts is unique to me, but the method itself is an ancient system of approach that belongs to no one in particular; it was a gift to us all. The method is *created by the method,* being produced out of its own truth and effectiveness. This ancient, living system is the heart of every religious, metaphysical, spiritual, and mystical culture throughout the world. I have merely attempted to explain this vast and incredibly intense process of conscious revelation in an updated and more universal way to save one countless decades or lifetimes of desperate investigation.

The rewards of the path, as stated by countless mystics throughout history, are too important and too incredible to pass by—if one has authentic teachings, it is like having discovered an extremely rare and priceless gem that must be guarded and treasured over everything else, especially over the things of this mundane, transient life that come and go like clouds in an otherwise clear, bright sky.

One's intention to treasure and ultimately embody these living teachings will also help overcome another problem often faced in the spiritual marketplace: the faith and trust one must have in the teacher. Where many so-called teachers have failed to attain the goal of the path, the vastly important teacher-student relationship has been all but spoiled. There is a great rift in what should otherwise be a completely altruistic and loving relationship where the teacher only wants to see the seeker attain at all costs.

The authentic teacher loves the practitioner in the same way they love their own child. If they could, like a loving mother, the teacher would easily give up their own attainments to see their child, the practitioner, gain freedom and bliss. For the common person who is habitually tied to the illusory identity, this is very difficult to understand, because the ego-body only gives when it receives something in return. But in the case of the teacher-student relationship, the only thing the teacher desires is the growth of the student into the best possible version of themselves.

Fortunately, the dark, egoic age is finally ending, and interest in spiritual teachings is growing. The re-emergence of authentic teachers who attain the full fruits of the path will ensure these gifts can be passed on to others.

So please understand my heartfelt intention: I do not want people to live in suffering, ignorance, or delusion, under the enslavement of the illusory identity, while forgetting that their essential nature is hidden underneath it all like a beautiful seed waiting to germinate into a bountiful tree of life. This work is a representation of my effort to give the seeker all of the necessary keys to be free, clear, happy, connected, and loving—the ultimate authentic expression of one's essential nature.

For those who do not know me, hundreds of students from around the world have spent years with me, some at my home and at my dinner table. They will all attest to my continuous aspiration to help elucidate this knowledge for whomever truly yearns for it, year after year. They are also charitably waiting to help anyone who needs it.

This project has been extremely challenging to complete, but all of the effort that has gone into putting this system together will be worthwhile if I can help just one person find freedom from delusion and suffering.

It is my hope that person is you.

I

THEORY

Theoretical basis for application of the practical method.

These teachings are complemented by ongoing lectures and discussions at the Drukama Treasury.

1

Approaching the Method

This volume presents the specific concepts and practical applications required for self-realization, the foundational process within all mystical traditions.

The important principles that could be expanded on beyond this basis are numerous and would fill countless pages. Additional volumes in the series offer fascinating and useful examinations of ancillary mystical subjects like liberation, the death process, ritual operation, the subtle realms, devotion and prayer, the creative principle, cycles and timing, consecration, supernatural faculties, evocation, governing forces, and many more. But one who is seeking radical evolution need not study the ancillary subjects. The foundational teachings regarding the method of authentic self-realization are all one truly needs, and those are presented within this system in full.

Part I of this volume is theoretical, offering an overview and explaining the terms, philosophies, and ideas applicable to the method. These chapters are the tools that reveal the basic framework of the problem one seeks to solve, helping one comprehend the path and the tremendous value of the attainment of authentic awakening. **Part II** is practical, the step-by-step approach itself, including the reasons behind each practice along with the general instructions for each application.

Both the theoretical and the practical are essential to the journey, so time should be taken with each. Do not worry if something in the theoretical portion seems out of reach; simply move on, and trust that the understanding will materialize in time as the awareness awakens and begins to notice subtleties that were not readily apparent before.

This method of realization is straightforward but intense, and it is made for the seeker with some traditional practice background; however, that does not mean the method cannot be utilized by someone new to the path. Regardless of personal experience, one should understand the overall goal clearly, and understand each application thoroughly before attempting it.

Part I Overview: Theory

- **Approaching the Method:** Correct understanding and use of the theoretical concepts and practical method provided in this manual.
- **The Intention Behind Realization:** The critical aspiration one should understand and maintain throughout application of the method.
- **Mysticism and the Intellect:** Examines the intellect as a potential barrier on the path and how to overcome it.
- **The Path of Authentic Realization:** General overview of the method and stages of realization, how the process benefits the mystic.
- **Emptiness and Awareness:** Explores the concepts of emptiness and awareness, how emptiness emerges, and why awareness needs to awaken to perceive it and bring about their ultimate union.
- **Phenomena:** Defines phenomena relative the method, explains how phenomena interfere with clear perception, how to approach them, and how they play a role in the structure of creation.
- **The Field of Perception:** Explains how the structure of perception is arranged and its influence on the path of realization.
- **Desire:** Examines the negative influence of desire and how it pertains to the path of realization.
- **Delusion, Confusion, and Suffering:** Describes the influence of

4

negative states and cycles and how they arise.

- **The Mental Aggregates:** How the mind creates an orchestra of qualities that seem to form the identity, what to look out for, and why distance is created between the aggregates and the awareness.
- **Elements, Channels, and Centers:** The convergence of elemental energies, pathways, and centers, and the effects of constriction on energy flow in the subtle system.
- **The Right View:** Defines the view and its importance for the mystic, introducing how and why it is held throughout the stages of the path.
- **Adjusting Single-Pointed Focus:** Defines single-pointed focus relative to the path, including basic application and adjustments.
- **Mystical Union:** Examines the concept of union, why it is important to the path, how and when it should be applied.
- **Mystical Visions:** The different visionary states and how they help exhaust even the most subtle habitual tendencies, how one prepares to use them, and how they impact realization.
- **The Practice Area:** Purpose of the practice area, how it should be maintained, and why it is important to the journey.
- **Physical Well-Being:** The role of the body on the path, importance of keeping it healthy, advice for remaining in a pliable state so the body does not impede progress.
- **Meditative Postures:** Importance of posture, details about the basic postures used during meditative practice.
- **Breathing Techniques:** Importance of breath, details about basic breathing variations useful for this method.

Understand these essential ideas well before applying the method practically.

The method assumes that one already finds intrinsic value in the authentic teachings and has established, or is at least in the process of establishing, basic proficiency with instruments like single-pointed focus, breath, sense withdrawal, and overall physical well-being.

The information in this method should be applied with caution; it is advised to seek the advice of a physician before starting a process like this. The powerful, high-level meditative applications deliberately influence the subtle energies, and beliefs or perception may be challenged as one's unconscious fears or habitual tendencies are uncovered. It is wise to seek help from experts, as many potential issues are circumvented through accurate and timely instruction. Even minute errors resulting from misunderstanding the method can draw the path out; obtain assistance to avoid accidentally making the path longer or more difficult than it needs to be.

The practices and concepts included in this workbook are of an advanced nature and were written in a direct but abbreviated way; the text is meant to be used in conjunction with the ongoing lectures, worldwide group, and one-on-one aid provided at the Drukama Treasury. This volume is used as a study guide within the supportive interactive learning environment where practitioners receive qualified guidance on each topic. One entering this system with no experience can still progress through the method with help from the general practice community, so do not hesitate to reach out to the group for assistance with the basics or for help determining readiness.

This book could also be used on its own by one who is familiar enough with the specific methods provided; we just do not recommend it. There are good reasons behind the longstanding tradition of seeking out experienced teachers, guides, and mentors in the mystical community. Access to someone who is skilled in recognizing the tricks of the egoic self-construct, who can clearly elucidate the teachings, and who is both willing and available to help navigate this challenging journey is invaluable. Without expert help, it is extremely difficult to reach the goal of overcoming the egoic identity that shrouds the awareness; the mystic wishing to successfully negotiate the path must seek out clear direction along the way.

The *experience* of realization cannot be taught, because it lies beyond dualistic perception. Realization itself is unexplainable; it cannot be communicated about in plain language. However, when the method is properly understood and applied, it begins to reduce the disruptive *noise* (distraction or disturbance) clouding one's awareness; this gradually brings about the actual state of awakened awareness in one's own direct experience.

The practical portion of this method includes indicators for tracking progress. For example, application of the visionary practices influences one's sleep states, where certain indicators make it clearer that one has been successful in the practice and when to move on to the next stage. Various signs and stages of visions in one's waking, dreaming, and deep sleep states indicate that negative habitual tendencies are being eliminated. Indicators also mark one's positive advancement toward awakening awareness. The eventual union of awakened awareness with authentic emptiness is what seals the effortlessly maintained self-realized state of perception.

The exalted states that are described may seem impossible to attain, especially if one is new to mysticism, and this is exactly the reason for offering the precise, practical means for reaching them. One who works through the steps in this manual and takes advantage of the companion lectures can naturally and automatically awaken the conscious clarity required to perceive the subtle states that lead to breakthrough (realization). But this process takes time, and patience is vital for success.

It is important to remember that prior to breakthrough, one will still be mistakenly entangling with the identity-body's endless desires and its many attractions and aversions. Running here and there trying to fulfill seemingly important goals will not bring success; exhaustive outward searching only makes one a slave to the needs of the body. There is nothing wrong with the body having desires or being attracted to pleasure and avoiding pain, but one will come to know that pains and pleasures are never really satisfied or resolved; it is the unconscious commingling between the identity-body and the essential nature that causes the continual cycles of confusion and suffering. When one makes corrections to these entanglements by becoming wakeful to them, one is free to explore the subtle aspects of awareness and investigate the root cause of all such phenomena that come into this world from deep within the field of perception.

The core purpose of the path of self-realization is to radically adjust perception. This is certainly no easy task, but with the combination of authentic teachings, a genuine teacher who has already attained it, a supportive group working to attain it, and dedicated persistence with strong, heartfelt desire, anyone, regardless of age, race, creed, gender, or intellectual prowess can understand and achieve it.

This process of awakening is also radical—it attempts to reveal all of one's habitual tendencies (unconscious attachments to desires). They are brought to the surface to be examined wakefully, no longer repressed into the subconscious where they can be ignored. Though all methods of realization involve the same underlying universal application, the mystical path can be approached differently based on the seeker's needs. Pace and degree, from gradual and gentle to fast and intense, depend on a number of factors including one's previous efforts, habitual history, external timing, and ability to comprehend and commit to the process. One's ideal approach is usually determined with the help of a qualified teacher. Readers of this book may have already been drawn to undertake an intense approach to awakening; nothing happens by chance. But regardless of personal circumstances, the goal is always the same: to unite insight in emptiness, achieving blissful direct knowledge of the field where all transient phenomena rise and fall.

The concepts and method may be difficult to absorb at first, especially if one is new to spirituality or traditional forms of practice. Follow the steps carefully, and the process will work, but take whatever time is needed to work through each stage without struggling with any of the principles.

The theoretical chapters do not need to be grasped all at once. They are meant to be digested over time and used as tools that are returned to again and again to be sharpened along the entire path of realization, and new meaning can be discovered in each of the concepts as one advances.

The practical portion includes important step-by-step instructions. While these chapters are meant to be followed in sequence for the purpose of self-realization, one's personal path might not be linear. It is not uncommon to revisit earlier practices for refinement before taking on more advanced applications. In fact, it may be necessary.

One should never try to leap ahead without fulfilling the previous requirement; skipping steps or cutting corners breaks down the effectiveness of the very instruments one is trying to enhance, and one must return to the place that was previously rushed through.

This learning process is unique, and at times, it may even seem impossible to complete. But when the text is approached with the right attitude, and any concepts that appear contradictory or seem to raise misunderstanding are left aside to unfold naturally, a progressive deepening occurs in which the same ideas, concepts, and practical methods gradually open. Approaching the method with patience and diligence leads to the dawning of inherent and relevant wisdom; over time, one can understand more clearly, apply more effectively, and see the path in penetrative new ways. The ideas, like seeds, germinate over time and sprout as one advances and gains perspective. Much of what is taught here takes on new meaning as the awareness continues to awaken and the relationship with understanding blossoms.

It is critical to refrain from positive or negative self-judgment, analysis, or assumption, and from trying to guess at progress markers along the way; remember, the full path cannot be seen from the deluded state. The subject cannot evaluate itself while the perception is still influenced by unconscious misidentification and self-referencing. If serious questions arise, seek the advice of a qualified teacher who can make a proper assessment and offer suggestions to help ensure there is no unintentional personal bias at play.

Do not allow worry or doubt to take root, and do not take perceived setbacks as indicators that the system should be abandoned. Simply take the path one day at a time, and know that when conditions are ripe, it will bear fruit.

2

The Intention Behind Realization

People around the world are in desperate need of authentic connection. One in the ordinary state experiences self, others, and the environment through unconscious filters adopted at every stage of development. People are unable to connect without interference from these filters, and humanity's difficulties arise through the resulting misunderstandings. Misunderstanding breeds division, division creates conflict, and conflict inevitably leads to acts of control, war, and cruelty.

Many approach the path of self-realization seeking a more profound and clear personal experience, but the mystic knows that personal revelation of the extraordinary state, where the perception is no longer bound by unconscious influences, has even greater implications for the world.

Misunderstanding arises as the once-pure awareness becomes sullied and coated in ignorance, continually grasping toward and identifying with what comes and goes in the field of experience. Moment-by-moment, over a lifetime, thousands of elaborations become entangled with the awareness and strengthen the misidentification. The awareness falls farther into the delusion of *being* the egoic identity, and it takes on the body's intrinsic suffering and lack.

To attempt correction of every misunderstanding and misidentification by attending to attachments independently would take countless eons. The subtle roots of the disturbances of the egoic identity reside in the habitual entanglement of the misidentified awareness with the identity-body, and these roots branch out into endless fruits.

Through proper application of the method, overall distance is established from the multitude of elaborations, effectively curing the misidentification. Without this entanglement, the roots of the branching attachments are effectively cut away, and the entire process breaks apart to free the awareness to return to its clear, extraordinary state where everything is seen authentically, as it is.

Becoming truly conscious of oneself and curing the underlying attachments that cloud perception is freeing; without entanglements to the egoic identity-body, one becomes naturally inclusive and understanding, acting in much more harmonious and compassionate ways, without bias. This free, natural, and clear compassion is the key to ending strife, war, and systems of control in this world; nothing else will solve the global conflicts and hostilities that have continued since the dawn of time.

If people continue to look outward for solutions to what are actually internal problems, there will be no end to conflict. If we can make the necessary changes without delay, our situation will improve, but if we fail to seize this opportunity to evolve, things will certainly get worse for us all. The solution is the revelation of conscious perception. This is the only effective tool for change, and humanity must embrace it quickly.

Imagine what the most important principle for the evolution of humanity might be, to end the ongoing suffering, misunderstanding, and disconnection. Might there be more benefit in becoming smarter, or more emotional, or more physical, or more connected? The intellect can seek to understand how things operate and suggest changes based on the findings, but throughout history, even intellectual giants have been unable to significantly effect conscious perception, and their work has not truly brought people closer together. Emotions may represent the spirit of life within us all, but without authentic understanding, their expression is chaotic; emotions wielded by an unconscious awareness fluctuate between love and hate. Extending physical life and attempting to create a healthier living experience for people around the globe has not helped overcome the lack of connection or the outright division and intolerance prevalent in the world today.

None of these outward efforts have borne fruit. Overcoming the problem means looking within, from a radically different perspective, to understand how the self and the world functions in a clearer, more conscious way. Individuals must be helped to discover firsthand how perceptions are skewed with self-bias and unconscious misunderstanding, and they must be taught how to remedy these issues immediately.

The core purpose of the path of self-realization is to adjust one's perception in a profound way. This is often likened to waking from a dream; however, modern use of the term "awakening" falls short of the actual experience. One might feel awake, and profess to be awake, while still feeling obligated to invest and defend in continual self-generated dramas, crises, calamities, and other abstracted conceptualizations about the identity. This unconscious behavior is driven by a confused and faulty perception; one who is still bound by habitual entanglement to self is certainly not awakened in the mystic's meaning of the term.

The true and ancient meaning of *awakening* is a complete and total break-through from ordinary perception into a condition that transcends expression, a complete paradigm shift so radical that thousands of mystics throughout the ages have dedicated their lives to proclaiming its benefits.

While it is true that hundreds of subtle forces could be employed by the awakened mystic to influence the reality to suit one's own agenda, such aims

13

fall short of the goal. The point of awakening is to reveal how subtle forces are causing one to be unconsciously shallow, selfish, dominating, and fearful, disconnecting from others rather than uniting with them. One who awakens releases subtle attachments and is no longer influenced by the filters and selfish habits associated with the egoic identity. Having overcome bias at the root level and transcended the ordinary state, one is reconnected and returns to a spontaneous illuminated perception that is no longer hindered by the lag generated from fear and mental obscurations. One is free to see things as they are.

A uniting intention should be held while one aspires to change the un-conscious relationship with the identity-body; its combined physiological, emotional, and mental processes are the very tools one uses to explore and experience this reality. If one is not even aware of how these basic processes function, one is not fit to perform important functions that affect others within society; one without access to vital, inherent wisdom unconsciously propagates more delusion, confusion, and suffering among the people with every decision and interaction.

The path of realization is crucial in this era. It is the last hope humanity has to change and reconnect, to drop the deeply rooted and unconscious self-bias that has been driving people to segregate, fear, and assert control over others. There is no other way to overcome this collective challenge; it is up to each of us to take on this responsibility before it is too late.

Endless tomorrows descend, and with them, endless excuses; there is never enough time, and one never finds the right circumstances. The cycle trapping one in the seemingly endless suffering of death and rebirth is already happening every moment, every hour, every day, every week, every month, every year, and every decade, not just at the end of life. For one who continues to ignore the constant warnings and fails to disentangle from the transient, the eternal remains concealed, and the door to liberation remains closed.

One who aspires to reveal the essential nature must recognize that this is no ordinary work. For the true seeker, it is the only work. What could be more important? The mystic knows that with quality and quantity of effort, it is possible to overcome the cycle within this very lifetime.

But this is the hero's journey, so while it is possible, it may not be easy. One who decides to set out on this inward path will need support, allies, and clear instruction. Whether one finds that companionship and support within our school or elsewhere, it is important to find it without delay.

The time to begin, or to continue, is now; there is no time to waste, and any other action prior to realization is impotent. The results of investment in the rising and falling phenomena of this world are apparent. One can instead make a life-saving investment in the treasure of the teachings, embodying them and carrying them forward so that others may also be free.

As the previously concealed applications for this process of realization are revealed more widely, their value may at first be underrated, but as more and more seekers adopt the method and see the fruits, these practical instructions have the potential to change the world.

3

Mysticism and the Intellect

P opular interest in spirituality has grown rapidly over the last century, and with that interest, more and more speculative ideas about the path of self-realization have emerged. From New Age notions of communing with interdimensional beings, hunting demons, or summoning and commanding angelic demigods, to fanciful beliefs about magick and ritual orders, one can find a seemingly endless variety of rumors, proposals, and assertions regarding what mysticism might be, or how realization might be attained and for what purpose it might be sought.

Most of these so-called systems leave the difficult journey of becoming aware of what one truly is, which is coupled with the intense process of recognizing and breaking away from the egoic identity, as an afterthought.

But to believe that one can stand up in one's current unconscious egoic condition and somehow command the supra-intelligent governing forces that maintain the underlying structure of creation, or that one can engage in intellectual discussion with entities whose knowledge spans beyond this dimension is just childish. To forgo one's own process of evolution and instead demand that the system itself, or the higher, more intelligent cosmic being, is what must evolve or change is the height of egoism and ignorance. How can one who is not even clear about who they are, how they got here, or where they are going when they leave possibly feel entitled and empowered to tell the rest of the universe how to rightly act?

If it were possible for one to force entry into the higher realms of reality where these more purified beings reside simply by making wishes or reciting incantations, one could go there right now; there would be no reason to wait around here on Earth. To move between the realms of reality, one's qualities must change to match the realm one wishes to occupy, not the other way around. The very reason one has already found residence on Earth, the realm of dualism and egoic reception, is because one's qualities match those of this system. Only a change in one's own consciousness will bring about adhesion to the higher dimensions of consciousness; there is no way around this law.

The mystic understands that entry into the higher, more refined dimensions requires an evolution in consciousness, in the awareness of who one really is. One is not seeking to destroy the identity, the ego, or any part of the body-mind; to ascend, one only needs to undo the unconscious relationship that entangles the awareness with the reifying identity.

This unconscious relationship, the entanglement, is what leads to continual separation, delusion, confusion, and suffering. One must find a way to detach from the dualistic perception that insists all things are independent. One who undertakes the process of authentic awakening learns that there is much more to life than the limited experience of the transient identity.

Direct, experiential knowledge is what helps to change one's qualities from ignorant, deluded, and filled with suffering to illuminated, clear, and filled with grace. Instead of selfishly taking for the sake of taking, one becomes sensitive and responsive to the larger, more integrated and inclusive view. An inclusive perception of reality allows one to effortlessly migrate into the higher domain to connect with beings who also live by this integrated, and interdependent view.

This sort of evolution is only possible through intense investigation and full understanding of oneself. For so long as one continues to conflate the positions of perceiver, perceiving, and perceived, confusing the essential nature with temporal illusory phenomena, one suffers and remains lost. One residing in this fallen state is not fit for the kingdom of heaven.

Overcoming the self is not about ignoring the body, ignoring the body's energies, or ignoring the self. The authentic path of realization brings about evolution through knowledge—true knowledge of (one)self. This is not a shallow and inconsequential intellectual understanding; it is direct experiential knowledge, won by discovering the nature of oneself through the deepest investigation into the source of one's being. To reach authentic attainment, one must thoroughly *know thyself* through personal, direct experience of the cause of all of the effects, knowing the root of the tree's fruits, so to speak.

With direct experience of the subtle causal layer of the structure of creation, one becomes conscious of what was previously concealed by unconsciousness, and thus is freed from the ignorant misidentification of who one is, how one operates, and how one perceives reality and themselves. It is only through the universal process of authentic spiritual self-realization that one can find true and lasting benefit; anything without this important core approach lacks integrity and will fail to produce the desired results. There is no other way, regardless of how cleverly it is presented or how entertaining it appears. To perceive changes, one must change perception; it is that simple.

Authentic mysticism investigates the nature of perception and the structure of creation it resides within. Real mysticism has nothing to do with blind faith, belief, dogma, morality, or ethics—it is only about one's own personal exploration and the direct experience that results from it. This exploration, the investigation of the mind, leads one out of the shadows of confusion, delusion, and suffering, and into a complete and sustained awakening.

This manual contains the theories and practical applications required for such an investigation, but before approaching any method like this, one should begin to examine and overcome some of the initial assumptions, misunderstandings, and doubt about the value and process of the path of self-realization.

One sets out on the mystical path as all seekers do, not realizing that the ordinary mind is already filled with deeply concealed bias and misunderstanding of the system and its process. The dualistic perception misunderstands phenomena as good or bad, right or wrong, black or white, continually confusing the awareness into reorienting toward its attachment to the identity. Phenomena are more than just one's thoughts, notions, judgements, conceptualizations, projections, and discriminations; they are also one's feelings, sense-desires, speech, actions, and cognition of the outside world.

It is very difficult to reveal the essential nature from the vantage point of the ordinary mind, even for one who has achieved some degree of wakefulness in daily life. True revelation involves the emergence of the extraordinary mind (of emptiness), which is beyond ordinary description. Vast and incomprehensible, the extraordinary mind unifies with the source of all phenomena. In this merged state, the entire perception of reality intensifies, radicalizes, and becomes ever-present in an incredibly spontaneous and authentic way that is completely unfettered by the delays of lagging mental elaborations.

Many people are willing to accept what has not been perceived directly, but this is blind faith. The opposite is true for the mystic. Before deeper forms of mysticism can be implemented, one must gain firsthand experience of the self as a transient and dynamic structure, and of the awareness as unchanging and infinite.

These realizations cannot occur through intellectual or imaginary endeavors, and they cannot be effectively explained; they must emerge through one's own direct experience. It is only through these authentic experiences that can one proceed to a more intense and thorough exploration of the subtle dimensions. This is always the case—misidentified perception must be corrected before one can attempt to understand the larger landscape of creation and the overall system of operation.

Fortunately, an intimate and personal realization of the divinity of the universe is not the exclusive privilege of a few saints, seers, sages, or prophets. It is a universal gift, given to everyone. No mediator is required for one to connect with the All, because the All is naturally present in every human. This gift is implied in the name *Emmanuel*, which means "God is within us." The mystic realizes this truth, and sets out on the journey toward the revelation of this divine nature inherent within all beings.

Before arriving at this path; however, the seeker endures many cycles of life which present confusion and suffering. Finally, whether it occurs in this lifetime or another, an epiphany dawns: the body's need to fulfill desire is inexhaustible, and repeatedly following the transient attractions and aversions of the body only brings repeated dissatisfaction. This recognition ultimately leads one to find the authentic path of mysticism, turning inward to investigate the nature of this confusion.

Realization is what lifts one out of these cycles and provides a wisdom that is unfettered by the discriminations of biased thinking. This authentic wisdom is a clear knowing that transcends dualistic perception; it is not shackled by the identity-delusion that would otherwise cause misunderstanding, confusion, and eventual suffering. Realization is not about suppressing the ego, removing the identity, or stopping the use of intellect or intelligence; it is simply untangling the awareness from its unconscious connection to the faculties that skew perception and limit one's understanding.

Because the process of self-realization is based in direct experience, it cannot be accomplished by thinking, talking, or contemplating. The same mechanism that created the problem cannot be used to solve the problem; one will have to *rise above* to find the solution. Thinking does not solve problems created by thinking. One must find a way to go beyond thinking, to the source of thinking, into the authentic emptiness which precedes and gives birth to abstract thought, which then becomes formed thought, which becomes feeling, sense, speech and action, and so forth.

The mystic is only interested in locating and solving the root of the problem and does not find much value in intellectualizing about it. The mystic knows that the culmination of the path is a personal experience of radical wakeful clarity and direct knowing, which does not require intellect. Talking about realization is not realization and will never lead to realization; one must do the work to remove what hinders the Light from shining, and there is only one way to achieve that goal.

When one finds and understands the cause—the root source within, who and what one really is—one understands all effects and causes. Trying to use the egoic mind to "solve" each problem that emerges by guessing at its cause or source is like trying to guess at the condition of the roots of a tree by examining each fruit after it has already developed and fallen to the ground. Instead, one can follow the method all the way to one's own single cause. When found, that knowledge immediately causes changes throughout the entire structure of the mind, heart, and body—one's personal tree of life.

While one continues to seek outwardly and unconsciously toward the effects, trying to solve the endless problems rooted into existence, one remains entangled in confusion and frustration, missing emptiness and chasing form (the duality of things). It is in the seeker's confused nature to try to understand the effects that are mistakenly perceived as the cause, but this fruitless search only leads to delusion, confusion, frustration, and suffering.

This insidious habit of mistakenly *looking out* into duality to find satisfaction is not really one's own fault; everyone has been trained to adopt this outward perspective through their environment. Our method is about undoing this common misunderstanding and revealing something truly extraordinary and wondrous; the center of the infinite sphere of awareness where subject and object are *not one*, but are *no longer two*. One finds this revelation by going within, through a specific process, to locate the source of the essential nature in an efficient way that most might think impossible.

But until that source is revealed, while this habitual and unconscious outside search for answers persists, one must exercise caution. It is impossible to evaluate progress or assess how close or how far one is relative to something one has no direct experience with. As the awareness draws further away from the identity-body, one might guess that the path would become easier; but in fact, the egoic identity is even more likely to revolt. The identity sees this distancing as a problem that needs to be resolved because the nature of the ego is to bind, not to provide space. So when distancing occurs, the identity-body generates all kinds of erroneous mental, emotional, and desire conditions in response. These conditions can appear to interfere with advancement, and this can feel like backward or unproductive movement to the seeker.

Instead of trying to guess how things are going using the same faulty instruments of perception that are causing the problem, it is best to follow the path without self-evaluation. In this way, one can avoid many common errors that would draw the path out endlessly. Remember to take the path one day at a time, and trust that when conditions are ripe, the results will bloom. Until then, as long as one is moving forward correctly and with good understanding, there is nothing to worry about.

4

The Path of Authentic Realization

Some aspirants in the spiritual community insist that one has nothing to find and nothing to do on the path. They say that one is already perfect and is already in a perfect, enlightened state. While in essence, these ideas are true, I have never met anyone capable of instantly realizing their primordial awareness by this kind of logic or reason alone.

Yes, the essential nature, one's pure state of being, is inherent; however, for the seeker, it is still shrouded by a multitude of self-serving habitual entanglements to the egoic identity-body, the temporal self-character. The ordinary awareness, fallen from its original estate, has mistakenly taken on egoic qualities that ultimately bind one to the state of duality and suffering, the transient and delusional cycle of death and rebirth.

Because these entanglements to the identity-body are hidden and have been continually reinforced over the course of one's life, it would be impossible to find and remove all of them by simply proclaiming it, thinking about it, or wishing it to be so. One seeking to reveal the awakened state of awareness and restore it to its original estate must first locate the true source of these unconscious attachments, and then make use of an effective method to recognize them and remove them permanently.

Some believe the spiritual path can be fulfilled through sitting in quiet meditation, being devoted in prayer, studying scriptures, or performing ethical deeds, often while waiting for something profound to arrive from somewhere else. Although these aspects are part of a spiritually healthy lifestyle, the authentic spiritual process is much more involved.

In the beginning stages of the path, before the awareness becomes awakened, it is still shrouded by the noise of the mindstream, and it struggles with unconscious perception. It is confused by the multitude of concealed entanglements that repeatedly misidentify it with the identity-body as it misunderstands and grasps at the rise and fall of transient phenomena in the moment-by-moment experience. The method examines this problem and provides the necessary steps one can take to correct the perception by becoming conscious of and removing the attachments that are concealing the essential primordial nature.

It is imperative to first understand the relationship between the "seeker" and the state that is sought along the path of self-realization. It is true that one is already in possession of the state one seeks. One's own essential nature does not exist somewhere else, and it is not something that must be attained from or provided by someone or something outside of the practitioner; it is one's very own natural, pure mind.

The problem is not that one lacks the state of realization and must somehow attain it. One simply needs to remove the obscurations covering what is already there so it can be revealed.

The problem lies with the unconscious perception of the awareness as it is continually misidentified with the identity-body in the dual position of the perceiver, separate from the perceived. The true estate of the awakened awareness is that of perceiving (nondual), but for one to realize that extraordinary state, the awareness must first begin to disentangle from its fallen state.

Entanglement is reinforced by the movement of disturbing underlying subtle energies, known as elemental energies. These energies define the qualities of one's transient personality (the identity-body), including the expression of thought-stream, reactionary emotions, physical sense-desires, and ultimately the way the external macrocosmic environment forms and shapes itself. The subtle elemental movement continually disturbs the entangled awareness, restricting the free flow of energy to it. These restrictions in the subtle energy channels are what keep the awareness fettered in the perceiver state.

The path of realization is the method by which the awareness is relieved of its misidentification to the identity-body through the reduction of the disturbing elemental energies. Only one who becomes truly free of attachment and obsession to the transient identity-body can begin to acquire the primordial state of unfettered perception.

The step-by-step process untangles awareness from its unconscious habitual tendencies. As it gains distance by cutting through and eliminating destructive attachments, it begins to realize its unconscious misidentification and awaken to the correct perception. When awareness awakens and is no longer bound in the position of the perceiver, what is revealed in the space is the field of perceiving, the field of nonconceptual emptiness.

The revelation of emptiness only manifests when one puts away attachments to the addictions of the sensory world, being *in it* but not *of it*, mastering it so that no unconscious entanglements remain. This happens by refining the elemental energies, the body's vitality, in conjunction with establishing and ceaselessly maintaining the right view. This refined state becomes deepened and effortless, beyond dependency on the egoic identity-body. When held continually, it leads to the revelatory experience of emptiness and the true and perfect baptism by the spiritual waters of grace.

Realization is the modification of one's mistaken dualistic perception of *this and that* into a clear and genuine perception of *this is that*, while also maintaining something unique. The mystic does not become annulled by the surrounding system or dissolve into an ocean of unconscious "oneness." Assurance has been offered to practitioners over many generations that one can indeed become unified while still remaining unique, attaining a rarefied state that is impossible to understand from the extreme and limited view of the identity-driven dualistic perception.

This is the exalted state some Buddhists call *not one; not two*. All external and internal phenomena, however they may be perceived, are beyond all modes of being and are therefore free from the cognition of existence and nonexistence, arising and ceasing, permanence and impermanence, substantiality and insubstantiality, and the conditioned and unconditioned. For the seeker who reveals the rarefied state, all bonds of projection, the bonds that were formed from delusion regarding all forms of conventional external and internal phenomena, have been destroyed.

This method provides the necessary steps to become conscious of and remove the attachments that conceal the essential primordial nature. Once most of the fetters are overcome and the unconscious attachments to the misidentification of the identity-body are almost cured, the awareness becomes stainless, spotless, and radiantly clear. This clear state is referred to as awakened awareness: awareness that is free from the attachment to the transient nature of the identity-body. Once awakened awareness is established, progress can be made toward revealing the nature of authentic emptiness in the second stage, which the awareness later unifies with to cause permanent realization in the final stage.

The deepest secret among the many concealed processes of mystical realization is that of unification. When entanglements are removed and the awareness is withdrawn from the identity-body, what is left is the pure, radiantly clear essential nature. The awareness can finally perceive the unchanging nonconceptual field of emptiness; it is free to unify with its partner to completely resolve the problems of delusion, confusion, and suffering. The union results in self-realization, the pure extraordinary awareness which is free from any attachments to the transient self. The state of sealed realization only ever occurs through the deliberate process of union; there is no other mechanism.

The mystical states generated from the union of awakened awareness and authentic emptiness are beyond the ordinary mind. The unified state of perception is indescribable because it is beyond dualistic thinking. Being beyond ordinary thought, the nonconceptual state of perception is extremely difficult to discuss. The mystic may use *via negativa*, saying what it is not, to lead a practitioner gradually toward the goal, because the identity-body does not possess the instruments to perceive emptiness; it purposely resides beyond sense, feeling, thought, and the external world. The identity-body is only transient; the field of nonconceptual emptiness is unchanging, constant, stable and infinite.

To understand the perception of emptiness, the seeker might inquire: How does one perceive the space in a room?

Space can be perceived because objects appear. Without objects, one would have no way to show that space exists; the contrast is what is perceived. In a similar way, the transient "stuff" of life, the rising and falling phenomena, is what allows one to perceive the space (emptiness). The space is seen because of the negative, because of everything it is not. This is how "God" hides in plain sight, within everything.

However, perceiving space in this way does not mean one actually knows space; it only means that one has successfully recognized that space exists through the absence of objects. In essence, wherever stuff is not, space is. This is the initial recognition, where one starts to perceive what had previously been ignored. In the final stage, one comes to know the space directly through unification with the newly discovered field of authentic emptiness. These two stages encapsulate the entire path of realization.

The Biblical *fall* from the garden of Eden introduces the dual dimension of *form in matter,* and this separation is important for the soul. The contrast, the mirrored reflection, provides an experience that was not available to one in the heavenly realms; the experience is what allows one to return after having been translated into something more awakened.

Perception of emptiness is really no different from perception of duality; both occur when shifting positions within the field of perception. Understanding this is key. The fall refers to one falling from the field of emptiness into the field of duality. The transfiguration refers to one rising back into the heavens as something renewed.

Through experiences within duality, within the exclusive perception of rising and falling phenomena, one prepares to perceive what cannot be perceived by the identity-body through ordinary senses: emptiness (of self).

The identity-body has no way to perceive the problem or the solution. Because emptiness of self can only be discovered outside of the identity-body (the ordinary senses), a new instrument of perception is required in order to perceive it.

Emptiness (of self) can only be perceived by the (awakened) awareness after the awareness lets go of the dualistic perception of the field of perceiver; it must move away from its entanglement with the self and into the field of perceiving. Only when it gains distance can it acquire the special instrument of perception. The ordinary senses of the body can only perceive transient dual phenomena, but this new instrument of perception, like a sixth sense, can directly perceive emptiness.

By perceiving emptiness through this new instrument of perception, one can truly begin to experience the space in contrast to what it is not (transient rising and falling phenomena). And in time, as one continues to experience emptiness from a distance, the awareness begins to penetrate into it by way of sustained recognition until a full union of awareness and emptiness occurs and seals stream-realization permanently.

After the initial critical revelation, one refines and deepens awakened awareness of the perception of the field of nonconceptual authentic emptiness while simultaneously transferring it from meditative awareness out into normal waking, sleeping, and deep sleeping states. This actively bridges perception of the pure, natural, nonconceptual spontaneity of extraordinary awareness into daily life.

The method of bridging the perception of the state of clear light authentic emptiness with waking states of consciousness has many stages. Using the meditative state as a basis for establishing the stream-entry point (the initial point of realization), one then gradually integrates this state in more intense and powerful ways, through transference, until there is no difference at all between the waking states and the deeply illuminated meditative state. This is when the practice of seated meditation is discarded; it is no longer needed, because the realized state of radiantly clear spontaneity, without blemish, is maintained seamlessly at all times. The *stream-winner* has sealed realization permanently and resides in a continuous, effortless state of uniquely unified radiant clarity that is irreversible and unchanging, regardless of circumstances. This state is the goal of the path of realization.

Summary of the Stages of Self-Realization

1. **Establish awakened awareness:** Awakened awareness is the state of awareness that has been freed from unconscious entanglements to the egoic mindstream and the identity-body. Establishment of it occurs through practices of subtle energetic refinement and stabilization of awareness that help one make distance from the identity-body.
2. **Reveal nonconceptual emptiness:** Nonconceptual emptiness is the source of all rising and falling phenomena and is positioned outside of the dual perception of perceiver-perceived (seer-seen). Revelation of it

occurs through very subtle energetic refinement using the senses and special gazing techniques.

3. **Unify awareness and nonconceptual emptiness:** Through insight, awareness penetrates the nonconceptual state of emptiness until union seals the state of stream-realization and it is effortlessly maintained. Unification occurs during dream and deep sleep lucidity, where the most subtle energetic refinement is completed along with this final union.

Many books have already been written about various methods of releasing attachments and attaining self-realization. Some speak about kundalini yoga or nondual Vedanta, some about Hebrew Kabbalah, others about Kriya or Hatha yoga, and still others about Taoism, Zen Buddhism, Tibetan Buddhism, Shaivism, Indian tantra, Sufism, Hermeticism and so forth. Countless texts address thousands of ideas about the path, but few unveil the pith and the associated steps required to reveal the state that every seeker wishes to authentically attain: realization, and the liberation of the soul.

However, the mystical path does not require one to select from among the multitude of differing instructions and divergent systems, because the core process is the same. Their approaches were slightly different, but all mystical traditions sought to disengage the essential nature, one's primordial awareness, from the bondage of the delusion caused by its unconscious attachment to the transient identity-body. Once liberated from this misidentification, the awakened awareness is free from fear, sabotage, misunderstanding, and misidentification in the field of perception. The perceiver naturally returns to its authentic position, the perceiving faculty, in the nonconceptual field of emptiness.

With a solid understanding of this goal, and with careful investigation into the nature of the various approaches, it also becomes clear that the systems all revolve around the same central concepts of either *energy* work or *mind* work. On the surface, it might appear that even mind practice and energy practice are two distinct branches toward the attainment of realization, with one relating to how the mind is focused in wakeful perception and the other relating to how the subtle energy is enhanced to clear restrictive pathways, but in truth, even these two were never separate systems; they are meant to work in conjunction.

The awareness must be awakened to reveal and unite with the field of nonconceptual emptiness, and in order to reveal the field of nonconceptual emptiness, the elemental energies must be refined. Refinement of the subtle energies within the body is what awakens the awareness enough to begin its investigation into the most subtle root of the mind. And one's investigation of the subtle root of the mind is what opens the way for the ultimate union that produces the supreme state of knowledge about the nature of the self.

The Drukama method incorporates these two fundamental approaches in unison, working with the subtlest elemental energies of the body while simultaneously awakening the right point of view that allows for the proper investigation of the subtlest nature of the mind. Harmonization of one's elemental energies eliminates the disturbances that have been causing the awareness to attach to the identity-body and harm correct perception.

Because an emergence of harmony between the energy and the awareness is so vital to one's success, both aspects should be developed skillfully to reap the most beneficial results. To accomplish this process in an efficient way, our method encourages activation of one's subtle energy centers along with refinement of the five elemental energies. These work together to reveal the most elusive habitual tendencies at the very root of the mind using visionary states and dreams, and ultimately through deep sleep. The enhancement of the awareness as it turns away from its self-referencing state accompanies the revelation of nonconceptual authentic emptiness, and the union of these two conditions through insight culminates in a permanently sealed state of full self-realization.

This supreme, awesome, and magnificent revelation can only be known through separation from the unconscious entanglements to sense-desires, emotional reactions, and egoic mentation that would otherwise reify the dualistic perception within each moment and continue to conceal the potential discovery of this great tree of life which leads to absolute truth.

The great appearance is truly a co-emergent experience beyond the three times of past (perceiver), present (perceiving), and future (perceived). This is the fourth estate of awareness, where all phenomena, or lack thereof, become the universal continuum of unequivocal knowledge, of unadulterated wisdom, and lead to true understanding. It is like space pouring into space: unbreakable, indestructible, fervent in its persistence, and beyond contamination, decay, or dissolution.

Anyone possessing this wish-fulfilling gem has power over life and death, good and evil, and all forms of karmic hindrance. Realized mystics are beyond gods, demigods, spirits, demons, and all other sentient beings in the realms of form and desire. They are free, uninhibited by any laws or structure, liberated from control, and emancipated from the influence of all other beings in this realm or any other. Their divine eyes are never covered by the obscurations of other beings; like the spotless reflection of a stainless mirror, they radiate and reflect whatever they wish, whenever they want, without the need for effort or burdens, and without the requirement of anything outside of themselves.

The revelation of emptiness can be so exciting, breathtaking, and inspirational, and it can generate such a clearly radiant state of awareness, that many mystics mistake it for full realization. Although it is true that perceiving emptiness beyond thought or sense perception is an incredible event that indicates one's approach to the summit is at hand, the final stage of sealing the state through union is critical to ensure that it remains permanent without fluctuating back into the remaining attachments to the identity. Emptiness is beyond the discernment of the analytical dual mind, and it is extremely challenging to find words to describe it, so when emptiness does arise within perception, it is best to simply enjoy the attainment while maintaining the right penetrative insight without ceasing, until it is sealed immaculately.

Emptiness is elusive, but it is wonderful; it creates a childlike glee. And for the awareness, it resembles the feeling of being home, regardless of where the body is or what it is going through. Revealing emptiness is the ongoing goal of the mystic, not because it is the end of the path, but because it represents the most important revelation on the path. Once emptiness is revealed, one can be sure that all the hard work has paid off. The end is just around the corner, and the path will be much more organic and seamless to attain from that point forward.

5

Emptiness and Awareness

Authentic perception of emptiness by the awakened awareness is a key attainment on the path of realization. One's perception of emptiness is negated whenever duality comes into being—the moment the awareness is lured out of its essential estate, away from the condition of interdependence and toward that of the independent self, its perception of emptiness is effectively lost. So while the awareness is awakening by degrees, the mystic is also hunting for the revelation of authentic emptiness. This gentle and constant seeking of emptiness is woven through the entire path, until the great attainment of its epiphany is secured.

The term *emptiness* is only a simple label that points one toward this revelation of the field of nonconceptual perception. It is called nonconceptual because it is nondual (beyond the dual perspective), and although it can be perceived by a subtle discernment beyond thoughts, feelings, and senses, it cannot be characterized in any way by the identity-body's limited faculties of perception and expression. It is called emptiness because it is empty of elaborations, concepts, and notions. Being empty of qualities, it is the primordial wisdom; it is the extension or mirror of essential nature.

Emptiness can only be perceived by the awareness, and the type of perceiving is unique; it is not the everyday perception one is accustomed to. Emptiness cannot be perceived through the senses (taste, touch, smell, sight, or hearing) or through the emotions, or through one's thoughts, abstractions, judgments, notions, reasoning, etc.

Emptiness is the source of all things, concealed so that only the awakened awareness can come to know it. It is like a mistress, hiding in a secret field known only to her lover. The identity-body is only able to perceive rising and falling phenomena; it lacks the proper instruments to perceive this field of emptiness. Because emptiness is the source field for the very phenomena the awareness has become entangled with, in order to awaken, the awareness must first back away from its identity-body entanglement; only then can it notice the space. Once clear from the egoic identity, the awakened awareness suddenly perceives something that was always there, something that was only hidden because of the misdirected perception of the body.

Emptiness is not a new mechanism that one creates at some point during the path, though it may appear new to the awareness as it arises. Emptiness is always there and has always been there, like the space in the sky; it has just been ignored by the identity-body because of its apparent lack of value. Emptiness is the space through which all mental, emotional, and sensory desires come into being, live, and decay back into dissolution. Because of the many disturbances within one's identity-body, the awareness either does not value what emptiness provides or, more commonly, the awareness is so overwhelmed by its fixation toward the various rising and falling phenomena that it fails to ever consider it.

But emptiness, this very space in which all phenomena rise, live, and fall away, is not a valueless condition. The transient phenomena that fill and make up the sky, like the clouds, moon, sun, stars, etc., could not exist without the area, or the field, provided by the space itself. In this way, this space, this emptiness, is actually the most valuable condition; it is the source and basis for everything to emerge from and fade away into.

It is impossible to intellectualize the attributes of emptiness because it cannot be grasped with the dualistic mind. Emptiness possesses qualities that blend so subtly, distinctions are very hard to define in mundane language. This is why the mystics of history have traditionally discussed emptiness in terms of what it is not, or in elusive and ambiguous ways. Nevertheless, the challenge remains for the mystic to notice this unexplainable and seemingly empty condition. Imagine a bird flying in the open sky. It is easy to see the bird, the clouds, the colors, etc., but the space is also there. In a similar way, one moving through the world of phenomena might never pay attention to the vast implicit space, because it lacks apparent qualities. Even though emptiness is the basis of everything, it goes unnoticed by most.

Emptiness arises to the awakened awareness when it rests in a state of natural selflessness; a state that emerges when one is free from the screen or filters of the egoic self. Emptiness is first perceived beyond the senses, feelings, and mentation of the identity-body. It appears when it is no longer hidden by or buried within one's dualistic perception of senses, emotions, and thoughts. As one reduces attachments to the self that was impulsively grasping at this temporary phenomena, emptiness becomes more apparent within, in the field of perception. At that point, emptiness becomes a *handle* for the awareness to grip and penetrate into until a sealed merger results.

For the awareness to even begin to perceive emptiness, and eventually unite with it, it must awaken. Awakened awareness is awareness in the process of releasing from its entanglements to the elaborations of mindstream. It is wisdom outside of thought. It is devoid of discrimination, intellectual analysis, judgement, or conceptualizations of any kind; it is formless and nonconceptual. It is beyond shape, color, and structure; it is vast, supreme, and without end. Awakened awareness transcends names, phrases, and letters; it is beyond ideas, theories, opinions, and the mental obscurations of the temporal identity-body. It arises in itself and by itself in a way that does not require acquisition or accumulation; it is omnipresent and omnipotent. It is the true water of baptism, which is not the physical, dense, and gross representation many religions and spiritual groups would have the masses believe; true baptism refers to the washing, the spiritual cleanliness that comes from the eradication of subtle disturbances.

Awakened awareness is the supreme epiphany which causes revelatory experience through one's direct connection with the ultimate uniquely unified state of spontaneity that is beyond explanation and ordinary speech. It is the light of gnosis, the divine chariot that transcends life or death, good or bad, and all other dualistic notions held by the transient and illusory egoic identity-body. It is the great secret of the mystics, the awesome supreme power of true knowledge, the majestic treasury containing the wish-fulfilling jewels of great masters throughout history; it is that which every seeker ultimately wants to discover within themselves. It is the only true, meaningful, and profitable pursuit in the cycle of a mundane life otherwise filled with suffering.

Awakening of the awareness happens through reduction of the disturbing energies that cloud perception. As elemental energies are refined and become less disturbing, and as distance is made from the identity-body, one's awareness can more easily perceive emptiness as it is.

Conscious perception of emptiness is only possible after some extent of awakening dawns in the awareness. And a permanent, sealed unification of the two is only possible after awareness awakens to a greater degree. The progression is why some experience the stream-like condition of realization but cannot maintain it; they very quickly lose it again, falling back into a state of ordinary awareness entangled with egoic selfing.

Awareness can be represented by *Adam* or *Shiva*, as the stillness principle or the mind. Authentic emptiness is represented by *Chavah*, *Sati*, or *Shakti*, as the movement principle or the heart. Traditional stories of the split and subsequent fall of the once-united Adam and Chavah are allegories for the disconnection of the mind and heart. This disconnection causes the awareness to turn away from the field of nonconceptual emptiness (the garden of Eden), bringing about the emergence of the field of duality—the tree of the knowledge of good (this) and evil (that).

In the fallen state, anything that is not *me* is seen as *other* or wrong, as something the self is against, or that it uses, controls, manipulates, or does not care for. In the state of duality, the only truly important thing is *me* (ego). The dual state is exclusive, segregated, and divides between the self, which is considered precious, and everything else, which is considered worthless.

Awareness awakens as emptiness emerges in perception so that the two can inevitably unite together; this unification repositions awareness away from the duality of the perceiver and back into its rightful place of perceiving, in the middle. This middle view is the vital estate of nondual bliss-clarity perception. The perception is nondual, yet it also exists in all duality. Once emptiness is revealed to the awareness, it transcends the dual perspective. In this state, it gradually bleeds out into all of the phenomena uniting with it and understands, through direct experience, the newly formed perception. Here, everything is interdependently empty (of self identity).

The practical applications one uses on any path toward realization must involve this distancing between the awareness and the ego-self, along with the refinement of the disturbing energies responsible for the chaos that conceals emptiness from awareness. Once awareness has been distanced and the elemental energies have been refined to reveal emptiness, the last critical step is to seal them together through unification. This ultimate union, or holy matrimony of awareness and emptiness, is referred to as stream-realization or complete realization.

6

Phenomena

A clear, omnipotent, omnipresent intelligence known as *Light* occupies the known reality. This Light is what gives consciousness the ability to be aware; not only aware of itself, but also aware of all other things that seem to rise and fall in the field of perception.

Light is the term used to describe the source of everything that is perceived and not perceived within the universe, including the perceiver itself. It is not only the intelligence behind the design, but also everything designed.

The term Light also defines the substance sought out by the awareness through the identity-body. Seen from this perspective, Light is associated to one's attempt to fulfill any sense of lack, one's desire to attain pleasure, knowledge, union, etc.

With regard to our method, Light is another way to refer to what is perceived by the awareness through the identity-body. The designed *stuff* that can be perceived, what seems to arise into reality, is also what we call phenomena. All phenomena can be thought of as being generated by the Light.

Phenomena, whatever appears to the awareness, can be any thing or many things, existing in any form. They can arise as thoughts, notions, visions, daydreams, memories, identity, emotions, sensations, intuition, energy, sounds, organs, blood, other beings, clothing, clouds, animals, rocks, trees, smoke, sky, magnetism, ocean, fire, etc.; the possibilities are endless.

All phenomena are temporal, rising from the source field and falling back into it. Awareness is a fixture, static and unchanging. One's awareness simply rests as it is, while phenomena like thoughts, feelings, situations, and the outside world come and go from within the field of nonconceptual emptiness, the source field. In this way, one can relate phenomena to the movement principle and awareness to the stillness principle. As one begins to draw the two together along the path of realization, movement and stillness are found to contain within themselves the qualities of the other, similar to the well-known commingling of yin and yang.

Rising and falling phenomena can also be called transient or illusory. Not illusory in the sense that one is not influenced by them, but illusory in the sense that they are dream-like. When one dreams of being chased by a giant shark in the ocean, the experience is perceived as vivid and real, and one rushes to swim away in a panic. But in truth, when one is outside of that dream-reality or is awakened within that dream-reality, there is no water, no swimming, and no shark. As long as one remains in that transient dreaming state, unconscious and misunderstanding, nothing feels more frightening or real. But like all dream experiences, the dream-reality of the shark, the water, and the real fear generated from the chase are all based on an entirely illusory condition which is nonexistent from a position of clear perception. Once one becomes conscious and wakeful within the dream-reality, it suddenly becomes apparent that these experiences are only more transient phenomena rising and falling within the field of perception, illusory-like and all made of the same wave-like or motion-like substance.

Although phenomena might appear to be an endless series of pointless traps for the awareness to fall victim to, these arisings are actually an ongoing series of opportunities one can use to evolve. Failure to perceive opportunities to make use of phenomena to awaken the awareness results in the continuous cycle of pleasure-chasing and dissatisfaction. Like a revolving door, it leads to countless births, incarnation after incarnation, until one reaches a peak state where the confusion, suffering, and delusion are so great that one cannot help but begin to ask deeper questions.

The mystic understands that one need not go through all of this suffering. If one can come to understand the gifts nature is attempting to provide, one can move ahead of the cycle with deliberate and conscious evolution. Experiences in this world will reintroduce rising and falling phenomena until one eventually exhausts the need to return to the phenomena and finally turns to investigate the essential nature—the experiencer of these experiences.

This shift, from desire-seeking to desire-investigation, is a monumental one. This is where the lone person among the general masses stands up and starts moving in the opposite direction. This one has now awakened to such an extent that they become a seeker of truth. Others will not understand, and will not see any profit in this seeking, because they have yet to develop such a yearning within themselves. The world can be a very lonely place for a true seeker; they are a small minority.

The process of generating the qualities of a true seeker can be likened to what happens when one rides the same roller coaster over and over again. At first, the experience is scary and overwhelming, yet strangely appealing. Over enough time and with enough repetition, an opposite experience emerges: the ride becomes boring, monotonous, and uninteresting. This leads one to seek out other roller coasters that seem new, exciting, and inviting; but at some point, after riding hundreds of roller coasters, one stops this activity and starts to wonder what drove that seeking to begin with.

This state of stepping back and asking bigger questions is part of one's initial awakening. Instead of just continually desiring the experience of more phenomena, one aspires to understand why any experience is desired at all. One who is awakening begins to see the nature of the control and restriction that those who are still seeking the fulfillment of desire are bound by. One begins to investigate the nature of desire itself.

Through this investigation, one can come to understand how desire is formed, how it is used, and what roles the phenomena are playing. One discovers that the arising of phenomena is really an unintrusive system used by the structure of creation to bring each person to their own unique point of awakening.

Although the rising of each phenomenon may seem independent and original, one eventually comes to see all phenomena as interdependent, coming from one source and made of one material. As a single wave swells, moves, and breaks, it might be perceived as different and separate from the others, but all waves really express the movement of the same ocean, like rising and falling phenomena are expressed within the field of perception.

The ocean and its wave are no more separate than the sun and its illumination, fire and heat, or ice and cold. These are not independent things; they are more like the interaction of different limbs on the same body. The unconscious perception is what fails to see their unified nature and instead gets caught up in the mistaken dual perspective that *this is not that*. This is where the misidentification to the identity-body begins; this dual perspective tricks one into believing that the world is made up of many thousands of independent things, when in reality, there is just one source and its emanation. Many colors may flow from a prism, but they all come from the same source of clear light; in the same way, phenomena are ultimately seen as tools that can be used for awakening back toward the clear truth of oneself and the reality in which one lives.

7

The Field of Perception

The mystic on the path of realization must come to understand the interdependent relationship between the perceiver and the perceived within the field of perceiving. A union must be made between the awareness and the field of perceiving to restore clear perception.

For this union to occur, the awareness must first detach from its position of duality, the perceiver-perceived position. It must return to the field of nonconceptual emptiness, the field of perceiving where all phenomena are generated like waves on the surface of the ocean. Union is the heart and soul of the path, and one's authentic breakthrough to realization is only made possible by remedying the misidentification of the awareness and its entanglement to the position of the perceiver so that it is free to unify.

Any teaching which does not point to the practical means for attaining this truth has nothing to do with authentic self-realization, regardless of any claims. There is no way around the requirement; the ailment of the misidentification of the awareness and the identity-body (identity, thoughts, feelings, senses, body, and speech) must be cured. This process involves energy which awakens awareness to facilitate the release, and the release is accompanied by a radical change in perception.

To understand perception more clearly, it is helpful to first consider the concept of the sacred trinity (three, the triad, the triangle, the pyramid, etc.), which is embedded in the major religious and spiritual traditions. In Catholicism, the trinity is known as the Father, Son, and Holy Spirit; in other forms of Christianity, it is known as the omniscient, omnipotent, and omnipresent. In Kabbalah, the trinity is referred to as the One, Unique and Unified (All). In the Hindu tradition, the trinity (*trimurti*) is referred to in the gods Brahma (creator), Vishnu (sustainer), and Shiva (destroyer). In Buddhism, the trinity (*trikaya*) can be associated to the three spiritual bodies called *nirmanakaya*, *sambhogakaya*, and *dharmakaya*. For the Taoist, the trinity is held in the Three Divine Ones, which relate to the one (soul) producing two (spirit), two producing three (body), and three producing the ten-thousand things (phenomena). In ancient Egyptian doctrine, the trinity can be related to Amun (soul), Re (spirit), and Ptah (body). In Alchemy, the three principles are known as sulphur (soul), mercury (spirit), and salt (body). There is also the concept of the three times, otherwise known as future, past, and present. Additional examples of this paramount idea of *three* can be found in mystical traditions throughout history.

Our method makes use of this universal concept of the trinity to represent the mechanism of perception, involving the three key principles relative to the overall field of perception. For the seeker, the perceiver (the rising and falling phenomena that is the identity-body), the perceiving (the field of nonconceptual emptiness where all phenomena are born, decay, and die), and the perceived (the rising and falling phenomena that are observed) appear to sustain independent roles. But through the method, one comes to know that these are all made from the same substance (Light/energy). Ultimately, there is no difference; one only perceives apparent differences from a skewed perception.

Clear perception was altered over the course of one's evolution, beginning when the awareness first became entangled and commingled itself with the identity-body in the position of the perceiver. The ensuing unconscious association between the identity-body and the awareness is the heart of the problem of all confused perception; it is the cause of all forms of suffering.

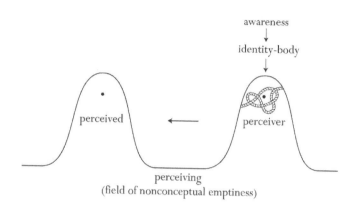

figure 1: entangled field of perception

Continued misidentification in this state leads to the formation of habitual tendencies, additional unconscious entanglements which strengthen the attachment between the awareness and the identity-body. The problem only intensifies over time, as the experiences one perceives outside of the identity-body, in the macrocosmic environment, subtly reinforce what appear to the confused awareness to be more unique and independently arising phenomena, separate from the perceiver.

Pervasive repetition of this dual perception of perceiver (this) and perceived (that) is what underlies the segmentation and division that creates duality in the physical world; although, just like all temporary phenomena, neither position actually exists independent of the other.

The field where all transient phenomena rise and fall, the field of perceiving, is the space the awareness must ultimately return to. Only through authentic teachings can one come to know the dilemma firsthand and repair the misidentification. When the awakened awareness is free to detach from the identity-body, it can perceive the field of nonconceptual emptiness through direct revelation. Revelation leads to the emergence of true and complete self-realization: the continuity of perception from the unencumbered position in the middle; the present, clear, and lucid position of perceiving itself.

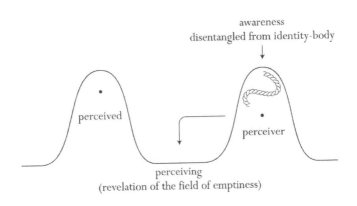

figure 2: disentangled field of perception

Once disentangled, the awakened awareness can return to its original pristine state, a condition without the dual-nature of the division caused by seeing perceiver and perceived as independently arising phenomena. In the Biblical garden of Eden, the beings experienced no disassociation or discriminatory judgement to cause misunderstanding between phenomena. In their state of primordial perception, the connection between each being was clearly understood, and the state was palpable.

It was only after the fall, according to the story, that each was cast down into a world of delusion where the interconnection between beings was seemingly lost. This is where the pristine awareness became entangled with the identity-body and assumed itself to be part of the transient existence, like the body; this misidentification became the source of all delusion, confusion, and suffering. The same misunderstanding was then reinforced through disconnected knowledge; the original, authentic connections were lost to fear-driven attachments to the body, sense-desires, feelings, and thoughts, all (incorrectly) assumed to be generated by the awareness.

The path of realization seeks to remedy the problem by reassociating the awareness away from its misidentification to the identity-body and back into the field of perceiving, the field of nonconceptual emptiness. When the awareness awakens and returns to its natural position, it can see the true state of temporary phenomena, and when the awareness can clearly see that all that rises and falls is of the same substance, the value of that phenomena is greatly reduced.

When the awakened awareness is freed from its entanglement and is united with the field of nonconceptual emptiness, this reassociation causes a direct reconnection to the infinite intrinsic essential nature of the awareness. The awareness becomes aware of its connection with the All; it knows that it is beyond the stages of living and dying. This realized state of perception transcends fear, doubt, delusion, confusion, and suffering.

For one in this new perception, where all phenomena are clearly seen as equal and transient in nature, a true understanding of life and death, through wisdom, creates a much more lucid and reasonable experience. And because the awareness is clear about its existence and its own nature, there is no longer a fearful need to escape into another physical body after death, thus alleviating the need to return to the cycle of death and rebirth in this physical world of duality.

The entire process of realization can be reduced to the awakening of the awareness to clearly see its misidentification to the identity-body and the return of the awareness to its proper place of perceiving within the infinite field of nonconceptual emptiness. Anything beyond this main purpose has nothing to do with authentic stream-realization.

8

Desire

Desire is one's hopeful grasping at the future acquisition of attractive phenomena. *Aversion* is one's attempt to reject or delay unwanted phenomena. Grasping and rejection are both efforts to somehow make use of transient phenomena to enhance the current state of the egoic identity-body. But the mystic knows that alleviation of suffering is not truly attained in the identity-body until the awareness reclaims its true home within the field of perceiving, the field of nonconceptual emptiness.

The ego has no concern for anything other than itself and is entirely self-serving; it is like a black hole of selfish desire, because it is never satisfied. While the awareness remains misidentified with the identity-body, it continues to attempt to satisfy the constant flow of illusory egoic desires, and this leaves it caught in endless loops of dissatisfaction.

The awareness will never find a cure for the ego's ailments, and one can see this in the endless wanting and striving throughout the history of humanity. No transient thought, feeling, or sense-desire has ever been fulfilled, yet people all over the world try, year after year, to perform this impossible feat. This should clearly illustrate the depth of ignorance and unconsciousness in the world, and it should serve as a reminder for the seeker to stop wasting time trying to satiate desire.

The idea that any transient phenomena are ever going to sate the continual longing for pleasure in the identity-body is simply absurd. The body will never truly become satisfied by the fulfillment of desire, no matter how much pleasure one provides for it. When the body adjusts to the temporary fulfillment of one desire, it goes on to require some greater pleasure, just to find once again that satiation is only temporary. Running around, day and night, searching for pleasure or relief in an attempt to "fix" the body's ache and lack is an exercise in futility and only brings more suffering. Yet most people in the world are doing just that, whether they are conscious of it or not. Everyone is addicted to pleasure; this is not just the obvious drug users, sex addicts, and those greedy for the acquisition of wealth, power, control, and knowledge. Everyone is addicted to something, and confirmation bias leads to pointing at someone else's addictions or issues while completely ignoring one's own.

At some point, one wakes up to the fact that all of this searching, cleaving, and grasping at pleasures has been completely fruitless. Seeing the futility can bring about a sense of tremendous suffering; but that suffering can then motivate one to begin the search for higher self-knowledge. Until now, this discovery has only dawned for a small fraction of the overall population in each generation. But from this generation onward, one can expect to find a much larger group of seekers emerging, because a sense of overwhelming dissatisfaction is becoming much more prevalent.

No matter how many ways science and industry find to make life easier, innovation can only be met with more suffering; the growth of the ego's need for pleasure surpasses attempts to solve the problem every time. Because satisfying the appetite of the ego is an unreachable goal, innovations will never be enough. Without a radical change in perception, people will continue to be faced with tremendous unsolvable challenges. One can find many examples of this today, especially in the political and societal issues that are surfacing and brimming over.

Although food can nourish and satiate the temporary feeling of hunger in the body, eating does not end hunger, nor does it solve the underlying problem of recurring hunger. The pills one takes cannot grant knowledge about how to cure a disorder. The sex one enjoys can never fulfill the deep, ongoing desire for physical pleasure and connection. Money can never satisfy one's need to feel secure. Power can never soothe or explain the nature of one's fears. Desire, in any form, when it is fulfilled in the ways the masses are trying to today, will never accomplish anything more than creating more powerful desires.

People are beginning to realize that no matter what they do, no matter how much they attain or achieve, their bodies only demand more, in a never ending pursuit of fulfillment for the supposed lack. More and more people are burning out at some point in their lives, and this perception of lack and suffering is contributing to the highest suicide rates in history.

This sense of lack is actually based in the mindstream delusions created by the body's indications that something is missing or needs to be remedied. These unconscious entanglements with the body cause the awareness to associate itself with transient needs, and thus it considers all of this turmoil to be coming from itself. This is simply not the case; the awareness has never and will never be able to satiate the body's needs. But this can only be realized through direct experience; it is not enough to believe it or to have an intellectual understanding of it.

Desire in the body will not die; desire is part of what makes one wake up, breathe, want food, seek shelter, etc. It is a necessary driver. Disconnection of the awareness from the identity-body is the only solution for the problem of one's habitual and reactionary approach to desire. With the right alignment between the awareness and the body, one can live in a much more balanced and contented way; this is just one of the beneficial side effects of realization. Common physical and emotional desires change drastically once the awareness is liberated from the shackles of the temporal body.

Not that the awareness will stop giving to the body; that would be impossible. Rather, one's unconscious attachments to desires start to change and drop away. This causes a new relationship to form, where wisdom can distinguish healthier desires from unhealthy ones. The overwhelming domination of desire is no longer the only driver and purpose in life, and because of this new relationship, desire can also be pointed in a different direction: for self *and* for other.

In the previous condition, where the awareness was unconsciously entangled to the body, that entanglement ruled over relationships; one could only give for the sake of gaining something back. But a realized being, in right relationship with desire, can give just to give, for the sake of being helpful and constructive. This is where desire is used in the most profitable way possible, for everyone, inclusively.

One arrives in the physical realm, the lowest realm of reality, in a transient body filled with desire, separation, and lack. The purpose and mission of this short life is to overcome the selfishness of the identity-body by kindling the vibration of inclusion, intentionally drawing it down from above. One who wishes to fulfill this purpose should refuse to radiate egoism and greed, and instead maintain the intention to transform self-centeredness and exclusion into the possibility of inclusion and giving. The intention to include is not selfish; it brings things together instead of forcing them apart.

This work is done not for the reward of pleasure, but solely because it is right, just, and good for all. The method is expedient for this purpose; it quickly exhausts the habitual tendencies that have forced one into unconscious selfishness.

9

Delusion, Confusion, and Suffering

D elusion and confusion arise in the perception from one's habitual misidentification with the transient egoic identity, and from the ignorant perception created by that misidentification. One's awareness has fallen out of its correct position in the pure perceiving state, and has become incorrectly entangled with the perceiver state.

In this entanglement, the awareness has adopted the limited perception of the identity-body and has become unconsciously enamored with temporal rising and falling phenomena. Its incorrect position within the trinity of perceiving leads the awareness to assume it is a part of the transient egoic identity, and that misidentification leads it to try to take on all of the unsolvable problems and endless unfulfilled desires of the body. The confused awareness attempts over and over to satisfy the body's continuous demands, but it ultimately suffers because the perpetual state of perceived lack can never be satiated.

The data collected by the mental aggregates in this confused state is also inherently faulty. The identity-body, in attempts to find and solve the recurring problem, focuses exclusively on the unique aspects of perceived phenomena. The mystic knows that in truth, phenomena are not unique; all objects rising and falling from the nonconceptual field of emptiness (the source) are of the same substance. The body-awareness entanglement is what fails to perceive the truth of interdependency; it assumes that some phenomena are positive and can potentially bring satisfaction (attractions), and that other phenomena are negative and will only generate dissatisfaction (aversions). These assumptions are mostly personal preference based on past bias, and are not necessarily true. In the end, phenomena is still transient, and the body is only ever temporarily satisfied.

The lack of coherence generates one unfulfilling experience after another, while the body drags the misidentified awareness around, endlessly trying to satiate itself with no hope for success. One seeks to fill the sense of lack perceived within, and must find greater pleasures to satisfy the same and greater desires. In this continual unconscious hunt, chasing attractions and running from aversions, the identity-body finds frustration, exhaustion, and even lethargy or apathy; it eventually realizes it has no solution to life's greatest problem: fulfillment. Continual hope of gaining fulfillment coupled with the ceaseless demand for *more* leads to one feeling lost, confused, and depressed in what appears to be a meaningless life of pain and sorrow.

After many lifetimes, an awakening awareness starts to figure out that something is wrong with its perception, and it begins to investigate other means of gaining knowledge, outside of the faulty identity-body. This revelation is like waking from a dream in which one has been eating a bounty of delicious fruits. When the dream reality ends, the illusion evaporates, and one realizes that sense of hunger could never have been satisfied by the illusion. Such revelations lead the common person to become a true seeker and begin to hunt for authentic information that can help remedy this situation once and for all. The mystical path reveals the evolutionary process of realizing the truth and ultimately liberating from the system that imprisons one in these endless cycles of delusion and suffering.

Imagine the various bodies one might have inhabited through countless incarnations in this world, like putting on and taking off different clothing each day. Who remembers what they were wearing at three years old, or five, or eight? In the same way that one discards clothing, one loses each transient body to decay in linear time. After returning to the subtle, one inevitably reenters the cycle in a new body, only to experience the phenomena of this reality all over again.

The way one's awareness enters a physical body in the world can be better understood by comparing it to the way one enters the dream state during sleep. The body is born and eventually decays away, but the awareness does not change. When the body seems to be dying, the awareness leaves it and continues on, unaffected, as if the body never really existed and was merely a dreamlike experience that came and went. After leaving the body, the misidentified awareness continues as before, moving from one body container to the next out of fear and insecurity. The womb of a mother provides a safe space for this awareness, which is still unconscious and in a state of potential, to shelter within.

When the awareness is awakened and unifies with emptiness, it is no longer hindered by the temporal, illusory, egoic self that was binding it to return to delusion, confusion, and suffering. When realization emerges, the cycle can finally end.

10

The Mental Aggregates

The identity only appears to be a singular entity. In truth, it is an orchestra of interdependent faculties which, like everything else in the body, relate with one's elemental energies. The brain uses the faculties of memory, ego (boundary), intellect, intelligence, and basic cognition to create the impression of a solitary identity, just as an orchestra combines the sounds from various instruments to create a symphony.

Each faculty, or aggregate, works behind the scenes in the subconscious, drawing from experiences and ideas based on past events and future projections. Without memory, intellect would have nothing to work with. Without intellect, ego-boundary (where *I* stop and *you* begin) would not function properly. Without ego-boundary, cognition would blur out into the world like the contents of an egg shattered on the floor. Without cognition, intelligence would have no way to learn and express.

All of these faculties are essential to the human experience; each works together to form the picture of what is commonly known as the self, and the environment that is seemingly outside of the self. But the mystic knows that in truth, there is no self to speak about. A song, just like the identity-body, does not exist on its own; it is the result of the perfect interdependent relationship of the instruments, working in precise harmony together.

Investigating the nature of perception on a more subtle level, one begins to notice the interactions between the mental aggregates. This growing awareness helps to break down the compulsive attachment to the identity, and one can see it for what it really is. Listening more deeply to the song, one becomes more aware of each individual instrument in the orchestra, and thus more aware of the fact that the impression of the song, as an intrinsic, self-arising, and independent existence, is illusory. The mystic recognizes the mental aggregates as interdependent parts that create a seemingly singular self, in the same way that trees, grass, rocks, dirt, animals, etc. make up what is recognized as a forest. It is clear that the forest is not a single thing, in and of itself, but rather a singular term that is used for a conglomeration of things, each interdependently unique.

Each aggregate also plays a vital role in survival and evolution. They serve important functions to keep one safe, productive, and consistent during periods of incubation, even into adulthood, and they are valuable at all stages along the path: before awakening, during awakening, and after awakening. In the later stages, the brain, intellect, memory, ego, and the rest of the aggregates become the very instruments one uses to become consciously aware of the instinctual nature. Although the entanglements toward the mental instruments are eliminated when realization through direct experience of the nature of them occurs, one can continue to utilize these same aggregates to create a meaningful life of purpose-driven expression and inclusive connection with others.

Because they are essential and necessary functions, both prior to and after realization, it is important to avoid judging these faculties as evil, harmful, negative, or worthless. Because these mental aggregates relate with one's elemental energies, they are also useful for the important ancillary practices discussed at length in Volume II, *The Luminous Eye of Wisdom.*

11

Elements, Channels, and Centers

Thousands of pages have already been written on the subtle body's energy centers, energy channels, elemental winds, bindu, dews/drops, seeds, etc. The objective of this text is not to regurgitate and fully organize all of those teachings. The following information will serve as a general overview of the channels, centers, and elements that are important to this particular method. A more comprehensive and advanced description of the network can be found in Volume II, *The Luminous Eye of Wisdom.*

The subtle elemental wind energies drive perception; they are the very forces that control one's thoughts, speech and actions, both in the moment and over the long term. The channels move energies throughout the subtle body in various ways, and can be likened to the veins and nervous system carrying blood and electrical current in the gross body.

The elemental energies are related to gross (physical), subtle (emotional), very subtle (mental), and most subtle (root energetic) conditions within the identity-body. The different elemental energies move subtle energy up (fire) and down (water), and in condensing (earth), expanding (air), or all-pervading (space) ways. Various combinations of these elemental energies produce widely differing effects. This volume only focuses on a few of the many possible combinations, including the union of the ascending fire and descending water energies for the creation of bliss-warmth. As one advances through the later stages of mystic visions, the internal structure of the channels, elements, centers, and seeds can be witnessed directly.

In the network of the subtle body's energy system, there are tens of thousands of various major and minor channels and dozens of major and minor energy centers; the centers act as major hubs, and the channels branch out into different directions for different purposes.

This method for self-realization only considers 3 major channels plus a few of the lesser-known secret channels, as well as 10 major energy centers which help with activation of the dormant inner qualities needed for full stream-entry. There are many other energy centers in the body that are responsible for various subtle functions in the energy channels. Examples include *warsaga, talu, kalana, guru, indu, hrit, manas, nirvana,* and so forth; dozens of these junctures are stationed within the channels at various points.

The elemental energies themselves are perfect. It is the restrictive energy channels that force disturbances within the system and inflict awareness with its misidentification to the identity-body. The effect is not unlike a short circuit in a largely underpowered machine.

Subtle restrictions are formed by the tensions (fears) arising from the misunderstanding and misidentification between the awareness and the identity-body. The spontaneous flow of coemergent awareness is stopped by the misunderstanding, one's dualistic cognition of rising and falling phenomena (this is good, that is bad), and restrictions are the result.

Restrictions can be thought of as tension, constriction, or tightening within the meridian (channel), which translates to constriction of energy flow on gross, subtle, very subtle, and most subtle levels. These tensions cause the elemental energies to be disturbed as they move through the system, much like water moving through a garden hose that has accumulated dirt and debris inside. The disturbances influence how the entire system functions and can lead to physical, emotional, mental, and pure energetic dis-ease.

One attends to restrictions by first refining the gross disturbances, then the subtle, then the very subtle, and finally the most subtle; this progression allows the revelation of the field of emptiness to arise in perception. Because each seeker is slightly different, authentic emptiness can arise for one at any time during these refinement stages.

During practice, one also learns to remain very still, motionless. When the body is motionless, the subtle elemental energies slow down and can therefore be more easily manipulated, internally, through intention and awareness. As the elemental energies are calmed through the removal of restrictions, one can settle deeper into meditative equipoise; this calm stillness allows for continued refinement, and thus the energies become even less disruptive. This process is repeated and deepened until one reaches the revelation of the field of nonconceptual emptiness; when emptiness is united with awareness, stream-realization is sealed.

The elemental energies are closely related to the major energy centers. The root center is related to the earth element, the sacral to the water element, the navel to the fire element, the heart center to the air element, and the throat center to the space element. The elemental energies also relate to the mental aggregates: ego to earth, water to memory, fire to intellect, air to intelligence, and space to perception (awareness).

When the centers are aroused and balanced correctly, their energy flows properly. The root-earth center's energy draws inward. The energy of the sacral-water center draws down into the body. The energy of the navel-fire center tends to ascend upward. The heart-air center energy tends to expand outward, to connect. The throat-space center energy is stillness; it fills and encompasses the entire infinite area.

The branches of these elements originate at the heart center and are related to the colors and shapes that emerge during the second stage of the mystical vision practice, indicating which element is predominant.

Each elemental energy is responsible for a certain supernatural quality; for example, air is responsible for reaching out, water for pulling down, fire for pushing up, etc. When these qualities are applied to various intentions and paired with their various seed junctures, the combinations can be used for a multitude of subtle mystical actions. Subsequent volumes in this series expand on these qualities and combinations.

The three main energy channels utilized in the foundational method are called the lunar, solar, and central channels. The solar channel is related to bliss, the lunar to clarity, and the central channel, where both solar and lunar unify, is related to nondual perception. Within the central channel are smaller and more subtle channels that can be referred to as central (central-central), very central, most central, and supreme. The subtler channels become accessible when the elemental energies are refined and awareness is awakened, and they represent greater degrees of nonconceptual (nondual) bliss-clarity. There are a few secret channels that emerge within the mind's eye as one continues on the path, including the branch channel that splits off from the heart, enters the throat, wraps around the ears, and moves up into the physical eyes. This channel helps create the connection between the heart center and the mind's eye, bypassing the physical brain and causing a direct re-union of the heart-mind in bliss-clarity.

The applications within this method refine the elemental energies responsible for overstimulated thinking, reactionary emotions, and dominating sense-desires. These applications are very easy to understand, simple to apply, and are effective without requiring much effort or in-depth knowledge

The five main subtle elemental energies constitute particular vibrations of the universal energy, just as white light in a prism breaks up into the many vibrational distinctions one perceives as color. Each of these five elemental energies contains a set of sub-elements. All of the elemental energies act interdependently in various cycles that repeat throughout the day and night.

When the subtle elemental energies reside in stillness, one's thoughts, feelings, and senses remain still and balanced, allowing the awareness the freedom to roam. When the elemental energies become restless, one's mind, heart, and body also become restless. For example, when the elemental energy of fire is stimulated, mindstream becomes very active. When the physical earth-like elemental energies are disturbed, there is an increase in impulsive sense-desires or physical ailments, etc.

During the cycling of the elements, approximately once every 72 minutes, each predominant element cycles through a series of sub-elements: earth of earth, water of earth, fire of earth, air of earth, space of earth; earth of water, water of water, and so forth. One can consider the possibilities in these combinations whereby a variety of scenarios might emerge, and imagine how a given disturbance might then influence how the body is thinking, feeling, and acting at any particular moment in time.

These subtle elemental energies are also heavily influenced by one's reactive habitual characteristics; some may be more intellectual, sensitive, or sensory-impulsive. The combinations represented in each person's unique elemental makeup are what constitute the positive and negative characteristics one can perceive in every human being.

Once the elemental energies leave the body at death, one's personal characteristics are dismantled; each being becomes exactly the same without the influence of the elements that had shaped and formed the personality. One's identity was created, and exists entirely, through the expression of these elemental energies. These expressions are reinforced by habitual tendencies, repeatedly fed through food, drink, sleep, breath, or directly through Light.

Beyond the unique configuration of one's elemental energies, there is only the pure awareness which observes the rising and falling of these forces. For one to experience a resounding calm state of peaceful openness, the inherent underlying issues with the elemental energies must be resolved. Simply attempting to bypass energy issues, such as by focusing awareness away from the emotions or the body, is not effective. Eventually, the energies overcome the efforts and one ends up right back at the start, having only gained a slightly more focused intellectual mind.

With the implications regarding the restrictions, the awareness, and the energetic power running through the identity-body, it should be clear that any method which does not attend to all of this—the refinement of elemental energies in conjunction with awakened awareness investigating the nature of authentic emptiness—will completely fail to guide one to reach full attainment of supreme and permanent luminous nonconceptual bliss-clarity.

Each elemental energy within the being expresses qualities that play into one's characteristics, such as general demeanor, overall expression of identity, emotional reactions, mental phenomena, and how one aims sense-desires in the body and through speech. While the mystic comes to know these qualities through direct experience, a very basic explanation of the five main elements and their sub-elements will be useful at first for practical applications.

The *earth* elemental energy condenses or draws together, causing all forms of solidification of the physical body like bones, ligaments, joints, skin, and more. Earth is directly related to the sense of smell. It also governs over one's desire for basic security, shelter, food, and over one's base survival fears. Within the earth elemental energy are four sub-elements called water of earth, fire of earth, air of earth, and space of earth. Water of earth regulates the moisture within the physical body and appears in the form of saliva, digestive fluids, urine, tears, reproductive fluids, blood, and more. Fire of earth represents the electric firing or impulses that drive the nervous system, digestive fire, body heat, synaptic processes, muscle contraction, and others.

Air of earth regulates breathing and respiration, speech, the sinuses, the hearing faculty, and more. Space of earth is the root of the physical process itself, the area out of which all other elements emerge.

The *water* elemental energy flows downward, just like water. As it sinks, it causes the next element in the sequence below it (earth) to come together and congeal into density and form. Water governs over general sensual desires and one's wants and needs beyond basic security, safety, food, and shelter. It is associated to the faculty of taste. Within the water elemental energy are four sub-elements called earth of water, fire of water, air of water, and space of water. Earth of water is related to physical desire, and fire of water is related to desires within thought. Air of water is related to abstract desire, and space of water is the root of desire itself, the area out of which all sensual desires emerge.

The *fire* elemental energy flows upward, rises, and is associated to the sense of sight. Fire is related to the formed mental aggregates of memory, intellect, intelligence, ego (boundary), and awareness. Earth of fire has to do with one's ego, the boundary that begins and ends the identity of *me, my, and mine.* Water of fire regulates memory, the impressions one stores as experiences are perceived. Air of fire regulates intelligence, the faculty with the ability to naturally and organically understand ideas and concepts. Space of fire is the cognition, the area out of which all other aggregates are formed.

The *air* elemental energy expands outward and governs over one's abstract and expansive notions and ideas; it contains the spark of intuitive knowing. Air is also responsible for the sense faculties of hearing and touch. Its sub-element, earth of air, is where intuitive ideas and abstract thoughts start to form before transforming into the fire elements below. Water of air is one's abstract desires generated through subtle intuition and insight. In fire of air, subtle concepts start to emerge into something more identifiable. Space of air is the root, or origination, of all intuitive and abstract concepts.

The *space* elemental energy is the unchanging, nonconceptual space that gives birth and gives room for the other elements to rise and fall. It is impossible to discuss the element of space in tangible, dualistic terms, because its qualities are unknowable. Space regulates what is called the God-Mind or the All-Mind, where something comes from (seemingly) nothing. Space is nonconceptual emptiness, the place where the awakened awareness uses insight to investigate and inevitably unify with that emptiness in perfect, resounding, radiant realization.

All of these elemental energies must be balanced and harmonized to relax and calm the reactive forces of the body. This harmonization is necessary for the nonconceptual space of emptiness to present itself, and for one's ultimate unification with it for the sake of supreme clarity.

One who begins the meditative path with fervency but does not harmonize the elements can fail to break though into the revelation of supreme awakening, even after an experience of profound blissfulness. Beyond a certain point, the continuity of a peak state can no longer be sustained. The imbalanced elemental energies simply resume the reactionary functions that make up one's normal "identity," and everything returns to the way it was before the profound meditative experience. There are many ways to generate exuberant subtle energies, but if one has not addressed the unconscious habitual tendencies, these intense energy experiences tend to ignite more sense-desire craving and lead to further entanglement. Danger also arises when a practitioner becomes attached to the bliss of a meditative experience and simply returns to it as a form of escape. For the mystic to continue toward authentic breakthrough, both circumstances must be avoided.

As one refines and becomes more conscious of the elements, signs of perfection will arise. These signs are typically referred to as supernatural, occult, or magic powers; but in truth, the faculties arise as a result of the harmonized tuning along with the increased intensification and concentration of the mental and energetic faculties. In other words, as one gains awareness of and influence over the subtle faculties of nature, one also gains the ability to influence them. If one can influence them internally, one can connect and influence them within others as well. This has been a controversial topic in some circles, but the influence becomes available to every seeker quite naturally as the elements are mastered.

Subtle awareness of the elements develops one's sensitivity to subtle vibration and to the higher faculties of clairvoyance, clairaudience, telepathy, hyper-intuition, and much more. These faculties are not magic, or some form of sorcery; they are simply signs that one's highly tuned sensitive subtle faculties are becoming active.

In the tantras, mastery over the earth element is said to be responsible for levitation, freedom from disease, creation of astral awareness, the ability to heighten one's sense of smell, and so forth. Mastery of the water element is said to remove fears and create supreme courage, give knowledge of the unknown and the power of astral travel, the ability to taste from a distance, and the ability to feel the emotions of others. Fire element mastery gives wealth, detachment, the ability to make an object *philosophic*, discovery of medicines, and entry into another's body (causing magical harm). Air element mastery gives knowledge of the past, present, and future; fulfillment of all desires; evocation of astral entities; the ability of psychic healing; inner peace and harmony; and complete compassion. Mastery of the space element gives knowledge of mystical matters, longevity, endurance without food or water, psychic projection, multidimensional consciousness (in two places at once), the ability to remove or add to someone's spiritual consciousness, to control and influence other beings, and much more.

Prior to the emergence of mastery, elemental disturbances still act on the awareness like controls govern a robot, pushing it forward or pulling it backward. These governing functions become apparent whenever the identity-body pursues or rejects pleasure or pain; the awareness unconsciously allows itself to be controlled by the identity like a dog on a leash.

To ease restrictions and make separation from the unconscious governing controls, one must learn to allow elemental disturbances to rise and fall while consciously abiding in the right view. The right view is the essential key to working with the elements in our method. The increasing distance that is made between the identity-body and the awareness as a result of maintaining this view while refining the elements is the progression of awakening.

12

The Right View

J ust as reflections cannot appear without a mirror, the clear view of phenomena cannot be perceived without the reflection from the field of nonconceptual emptiness. Primordial consciousness pervades everything through awareness in the same way the sun illuminates the solar system with light.

Understanding how to arrive in the right view is the most essential part of the journey of realization and is as important as seated practice. One must view all things as thoroughly undifferentiated, as both essential and nonessential. Like burning away the haystack reveals the proverbial needle, eliminating habitual disturbances reveals what is essential, real, and infinitely pure.

Before one can establish the authentic view, one must have the intention to form the preliminary view. This preliminary view is the aspiration to see things as they really are, to maintain a perfect continuum of radical insight about the true nature of rising and falling distractions that appear when sitting, walking, and in sleep. To accomplish this, one must understand that all phenomena are simply the play within the luminous expanse of pure inclusive empty bliss-clarity, revealed to those heroes that set a determined and established view of reality without wavering, without falling back into the delusional, conceptual, and divisive state of dual-confusion.

The naked, clear, and free view holds no individual phenomenon in esteem over any other. At once, without coercion or evaluation, it perceives all phenomena as inherently equal in weight and value, all made from the same substance. This freedom of perception, this view, is vast, open, and effortless, an unimpeded continuity of perceiving that penetrates into what is real—the nonconceptual nature of reality.

The colorless, unchanging, radically liberated, and spontaneously emergent right view is essential. Because all phenomena that rise and fall from the field of emptiness are made of the same material, the mind can be trained to loosen its compulsion to identify with the transient forms it encounters in every waking and sleeping moment. For one to overcome the identity-body's powerful addiction to the ever-changing state of phenomena, the view must be cultivated in waking, meditative, dream, and deep sleep states.

The process of establishing the right view in waking, seated, and sleep practice helps recondition the mind to stop endlessly grasping at and judging everything it becomes aware of. The view relaxes the disturbing conditions of the elemental energies that violently push and pull, thereby relieving all kinds of chaos in the mind, heart, and body.

The right view rejects nothing and accepts nothing; it remains in the middle with a free and clear perception of reality. This view only sees the play of the Light in a dream-like condition of present acceptance of all thoughts, all feelings, all sense-desires, and all outside phenomena; everything is free from elaborations, notions, judgements, conditions, abstractions or conjecture. The right view recognizes everything in the same way, seeing all arising forms as challenges from the system to draw one from that view, as tests of awareness to determine one's readiness for liberation.

Unconscious and reactionary associations with the ego's attractions and aversions pull one from the right view and lead to further entanglement by reinforcing misidentification with the self. Misidentification leads one to assume that the qualities represented are *who I am*, and that these qualities, whether favorable or unfavorable, are unique to the bearer. Fortunately, neither assumption is accurate.

This method naturally causes the upheaval of one's deepest desires, fears, and confusion. But the most shameful, embarrassing, repressed, and dark qualities of the egoic self actually represent some of the most important and often overlooked opportunities along the path. These aspects of the identity-body are typically so deeply subdued and inhibited that their very existence becomes veiled; they are habitually repressed into the deep subconscious layer of the mind, only rising up and out during intense moments in one's waking or dreaming states.

Like all phenomena that rise and fall in the field, these deep desires of the body are also transient; they are not part of the infinite essential nature, the awareness itself. Desires themselves are not bad or good; they are a completely natural part of the identity-body's process.

In the state of unconscious confusion and ignorance resulting from misidentification out in the field of perceiving, one simply gets caught up in desire phenomena and associates them to awareness. It is only one's unconscious entanglement toward desire that causes the misidentification and the endless suffering one experiences in life. Desires are merely something that the essential nature witnesses, and for one who is patient and wakeful, it becomes clear that attractions and aversions also come and go like the wind and are all made of the same intrinsic substance.

And as one continues to stabilize and deepen this view, those previously unwanted qualities, such as fear of attainment, fear of delusion, avoidance of ridicule, aversion to lack, and fear of losing oneself completely fall away.

One who rests in the right view becomes supremely vibrant, unconquerable, perfectly steady, extraordinarily cognizant, and is victorious over birth, decay, and death, because all illusions of impermanence and suffering have been vanquished. The perception perceives correctly, like an open blue sky, free from any elaborations or unnecessary abstractions, projections, assumptions, judgements, or conceptualizations.

Awareness of awareness is one's extraordinary perception which sees through the ordinary conditions of phenomena and turns back onto itself to rest in the immediate and present natural state; it refuses to expend energy on the useless endeavors that had previously entangled it into chasing shadows. This freedom of perception allows one to focus on what is most important: the view. The right view sustains itself; the view is what keeps the view going without interruption.

When the mind is free from elaborations, it can release its tense grip; it can stop leaping around to over-think and over-stress about what has already happened or what will happen—one should not be concerned with such things on this path. What happened is over. What will happen is not here. What is happening now is just the irrelevant passing of what is coming and what has come, just as it is. All of it is left to fly around on its own, without need of fear-based obscurations.

This view is not tied to the present, not tied to the future, and not tied to the past; it is holding each moment as it is: the dream-like rising and falling of the same substance in seemingly different forms. The same clay can be used to make a cup, a pot, or a dish; although they take different shapes, the base form is all clay. In the same way, all thoughts are made of the same rising and falling empty material. Emotions are just energy in motion. And senses are fleeting, here one moment, gone the next. The mystic skillfully realizes that everything is impermanent, and treats it all the same.

The key to the view is in equalizing all phenomena, getting used to perceiving all as a play of the field of emptiness, recognizing that these expressions of the All do not require one to over-think, over-act, or sensationalize. This does not mean regressing awareness into dullness. It means one is ultra-aware of everything as it is, seeing everything that arises in a more truthful, clear, and effortless way.

This correct view is how one releases the habitual tendencies that have been creating drama from each instance of rising phenomena. When one knows that all of these risings will fade away, as they always do, there is no reason to expend unconscious energy at each juncture trying to solve, discriminate, struggle with, or defend or attack.

The right view constantly holds the idea: "This is what it is," without wasting time and energy grappling with the mirage that is one's illusory concepts and transient empty thought stream. The view is simply one's calm abiding in perfect balance, just seeing what is there without unnecessary interruption or pointless intervention.

The lens of awakened awareness is thus cultivated over time, alongside the reduction of the elemental energy disturbances which have confused and entangled the awareness into perception of *this is not that*. Eventually, conceptual thought is let go of; it drifts away, and in its place is the arrival of the pure-land fields of naturally occurring simplistic brilliance. This emptiness is like the clear blue sky, and awakened awareness is like the sun radiating in the infinitely empty universe of Light. When the two of these inevitably unite, they remain in seamless perpetual unique unity.

Ultimately, the right view is maintained by one's ongoing awareness of the nonconceptual field of emptiness, which is like space pouring into space, or the sun rising in a perfectly clear sky. The authentic right view is lucid, natural, empty but clear, dynamically unique and alive, and at the same time radiantly unified. But in the beginning, one still experiences subtle cleaving when trying to maintain the view. This cleaving gradually falls away in time, if one is diligent.

The right view is free from holding on to anything, and this means that any tension, grasping, or cleaving to a state, even if it seems clear, still, or outside of normal mundane perception, is an incorrect position. Imitate the play of a small child: open, free, and inviting all events as they come and go, never regretting or noticing disappointment toward anything. Children innocently embody the wakeful and organic right view that should be constantly maintained. The right view is held open to everything that occurs without bias, reflection, analysis, assumption, speculation, projection, judgment, or any other state that is not pure, authentic, lucid, continuously spontaneous acceptance. The right view goes beyond thinking, to *experience as experience occurs*. This takes time to get used to, but once it is found, it will certainly deepen as the practices progress.

The path is holding and correctly maintaining the right view. In the view, the awareness is awakened, detached from unconscious entanglement, and freed from the dominance of the identity-body. The process is expedited by deliberate exhaustion of disturbances generated by underlying restrictions. This is called using energy to enhance skillful means (of escape).

Right view means constantly moving in the right direction.

- Right *direction* means beyond thinking, bypassing all thoughts, judgements, analysis, conjecture, abstraction, notions, and assumptions, and *remaining* in a state of pure radiant awareness. This is called bypassing identity and pointing in another direction.
- Right *movement* means constantly maintaining the intention that is certain this right direction will lead to the revelation of the field of nonconceptual emptiness. This is called faith, and making space between awareness and identity-body.
- *Constant* means never turning back (toward mindstream). One who seeks will find, but one in double-mindedness is lukewarm and will fail. This constancy is called rejecting death and accepting life.

This is the manner in which one holds the right view. Precise direction in conjunction with constant movement is the only authentic path to stream-realization.

The process of right view leading to realization is not what takes time; what takes time is one's adjustment to correct maintenance of the right view. Double-mindedness stalls realization, and the correction of it ultimately determines the duration of the path. Once one is convicted and aimed in the right direction, seeking is very short-lived; emptiness is immediately revealed for the potential union.

13

Adjusting Single-Pointed Focus

Single-pointed focus, one of the most vital instruments within the mystic's arsenal, is a steady and unbreakable stream of awareness aimed at an object of investigation. What typically inhibits this anchored continuity of awareness is one's attention toward rising phenomena that distract and interrupt the stream.

Maintaining continual focus on an object has nothing to do with strength or force; in fact, authentic single-pointed focus comes naturally after one makes certain adjustments to how one views and values the rising and falling phenomena in the field. While focus is held correctly, one is breaking through the misappraisal of the perceived content of phenomena, whether that is subtle energy, thought-stream, emotional reactions, sense-desires, or the phenomena that occurs in the macrocosmic field of experience.

When equanimity of view is created, things that rise and fall are seen in a balanced way. No matter what appears within the field of perception, it holds no greater value than the selected object of investigation. When the right view is established, one can maintain effortless single-pointed focus on whatever one wishes. This continual focus does not rely on strain, stress, or power; it just calmly rests on the object because there is no distraction important enough to draw the attention of the awareness away.

The problem most people encounter with the practice of single-pointed focus is that reactionary influence, or unconscious valuing, is reinforcing subtle degrees of entanglement. Even if one can generally rest awareness on an anchor by discarding other gross phenomena, it is impossible to overcome the subtle unconscious habitual tendencies that break one's focus on the object. The misidentified awareness automatically leaps to notice whatever peripheral phenomena are arising outside of one's deliberate control.

The confused awareness is unable to fully establish and maintain clear and stable focus on the object of concentration. One's lack of ease in this case, driven by ongoing disturbances on gross or subtle levels, creates an undercurrent of frustration within the system which results in further confusion and suffering. When one cannot rest on an idea, feeling, sense, or outside object to investigate and contemplate it, one is also unable to think clearly or concentrate well. The echoes of whatever mistakes are made in speech or action due to this lack of focus and clarity come back to one in the form of negative karmic consequences.

Fortunately, with practice, the tight grip those disturbing elemental energies have on the system can be loosened. Within that emerging freedom, one gains access to higher degrees of restful abiding, and within that emerging space a multitude of subtle experiences, previously unnoticed, become apparent in every moment. As the elemental energies are further refined, one's effortless resting concentration allows for the unveiling of aspects of reality that are typically missed by the masses. These new and very subtle experiences begin to fill in pieces of the puzzle, exposing concealed aspects of the creative process and hidden features of the structure of creation.

To ensure effective meditative and waking practice, one should understand how to adjust the view on the object of focus so that it is neither too restrictive nor too loose. When the view is too rigid, one's energies, mind, heart, and body become rigid. When the view is too relaxed, the anchor is lost and awareness is swept away by errant thoughts.

Whenever awareness strays from the anchor in meditative practice, following mindstream or body reactions, re-anchor using basic resistance breathing (ocean breath) with awareness in the belly. This relaxing breath is restrained, even, long, slow, and rhythmic; awareness follows the breath as it enters the body, fills the belly, and exits the body. Watching the breath, notice when the awareness feels steady again, then re-establish the anchor to resume the practice.

One can also tighten and loosen the view to prevent straying. Tighten by gentlly refocusing on the anchor when concentration becomes too loose or unfocused and the awareness begins to drift. Loosen by gently relaxing and reducing overly fixed or tight perception toward the anchor.

Skillful and constant adjustment allows one to feel settled, with the proper balance of relaxed, effortless, continuous, and calm abiding on the anchor. The balance achieved with use of these tools reveals how to comfortably and effortlessly rest on the object without strain or stress, and without too much unfocused, distracted, or wandering concentration due to mindstream influence. Tightening and loosening also strengthens will, so that overall mindstream is weakened and less distraction occurs over time.

One should be mindful of straying at all times. These tools are not just useful for returning to an anchor in meditative practices; they are also essential for returning to and maintaining the view in waking and dreaming states. To help cultivate continuity of the right view in the waking state, one can use tightening and loosening to diligently adjust whenever the mind seeks to attach to or avert from phenomena.

Subtle unconscious habitual tendencies are eliminated through the right view and the eradication of elemental energy disturbances. Over time, one's ability to apply the view and rest in complete calm abiding (authentic single-pointed focus) on any chosen object in moment-by-moment waking states become increasingly natural, simple, and effortless.

14

Mystical Union

Union is one of the key mystical instruments. It breaks down the dualistic boundary so that the various aspects of an object of investigation can be experienced directly. In union, the perceiver and the perceived merge to become one uniquely unified singularity, allowing the mystic to experience the subtle qualities of the object that cannot be known by observing it from the outside.

Attempting to understand an object of investigation through external, intellectual pursuits can only lead to educated guesses about the object's actual nature. Very little can be known about an object simply by watching it or studying it and making assumptions about it from those observations. To truly know something, one cannot be separate from it; one must *become* it, acquire its qualities, and work with those qualities to gain authentic wisdom about that object.

This union is a principle component of the mystical process of realization. The mystic seeks to correct the misidentification the awareness, to detach the awareness from the egoic identity-body. As the awareness gains distance from the egoic identity, it must also understand its true position outside of the rising and falling phenomena—beyond the seer and seen, perceiver and perceived positions—and it must return back into the non-conceptual field of phenomena itself: emptiness. The only way to seal this restored state of perceiving is for the awareness to unify with the field of emptiness, to acquire some of its properties and become like it, re-aligning itself by noticing the similar properties that both the awareness and the field of non-conceptual emptiness possess.

Union is similar to single-pointed focus in that for either of them to be performed successfully, some degree of elemental energy disturbance must already be eliminated. When elemental energy disturbance is eliminated, the restriction or tension of the entanglements between the body and the awareness is reduced. Within this reduction, the awareness gains ease and a more fluid ability to leave its seemingly localized position within the body. With this reduction in stickiness to the identity-body, the awareness can make use of single-pointed focus to penetrate into the object of investigation while also letting go of the shackles that trap it to the egoic self. These freeing conditions allow the awareness to easily unify with and adopt the qualities of anything it wishes to know.

Union and single-pointed focus, along with other advanced tools, are used to release the awareness from a localized condition into a much more expansive, inclusive state. This process of letting go expands the awareness into the non-conceptual field of emptiness as the object of investigation. Since the field of nonconceptual emptiness is vast, the awareness must also realize this vast condition. The awakened awareness and the field of emptiness must unite and become one uniquely unified singularity, unified outside of the dual-perception that was trapped under the influence of illusory rising and falling phenomena. Unification is what establishes effortless continuous realization, where all action becomes *action-less*.

Before one can attempt to unify awareness with emptiness, the restrictions in the subtle body must be loosened. The most prominent restrictions can be found in the energy body, the emotional body, and the mental body (mind, heart, and physical body). These three main restrictions have the most

79

powerful influence over the entanglement of the awareness to mentation, emotions, and sense-desires. The restricted flow of Light in these areas weakens the awareness, and this contributes to its mistaken belief that it is *one* with the more prominent and noticeable identity-body. To eliminate these major restrictions, one works on the subtle, very subtle, and most subtle elemental energies. When the restrictions are reduced and more Light can flow through the channels of the body, the awareness can awaken.

With fewer constrictions in the subtle channels, the strengthened awareness awakens to the direct experience that it is not actually locked into its misidentification with the identity-body, and union becomes possible. The elimination of elemental energy disturbances allows the awareness to see that it has other options, including the union of emptiness.

The method provided here helps one reduce elemental energy disturbances so that the awareness can awaken and inevitably enter into that union. Unification fully untangles the awareness and allows it to return to its proper estate in the field of nonconceptual emptiness where all phenomena rises and falls (the source). This adjusts the awareness into a new paradigm of perception, the culmination of self-realization.

15

Mystical Visions

The most important aspect of realization is the union of heart and mind. It is only when these resonate together in unified equality that one can effortlessly sustain the right view and perceive reality with true clarity. This connection between heart and mind is where nondual, nonconceptual bliss-clarity rises beyond the mundane and creates a state of joyful lucidity that attracts true wisdom, knowledge, and understanding.

The terms *heart* and *mind* do not refer to one's fleshy heart or one's material or egoic mind; they relate to the energy channels that connect the true subtle heart-mind. The link between the heart center and the inner mind's eye is created through refinement. There is no intellectual pathway for this to occur, and the connection cannot be forced through any other means; the purification of one's elemental energies in conjunction with development of the right view is what opens the bridge and awakens these two subtle aspects so they can become uniquely unified.

The heart and the mind represent bliss (heart) and clarity (mind). At first, these can seem to be separate experiences; yet when the two come together in a nondual revelation, bliss-clarity becomes one spontaneous occurrence. Bliss and clarity are related to awareness (bliss) and emptiness (clarity). When awareness begins to perceive the field of nonconceptual emptiness through the exhaustion of energy disturbances, wisdom is gained through the clarity that is revealed, and bliss simultaneously rises due to one's emerging freedom from mental noise.

The mystic vision practices in Part II are designed to help exhaust the very subtle elemental energies in preparation for unification. Through maintaining certain postures, the right gazes, the right view, and arousing the right energy centers, one's habitual tendencies are forced to the surface and eventually exhausted.

One who is established in the right view is able to attend to and uproot these habitual tendencies with no reaction. Intensification of specific types of visions shows that one is moving into more subtle layers of the underlying disturbances. As one continues the practice, the visions become harder to ignore, further testing the view. The subtle nature of these tendencies represents root layers of the elemental disturbances, and when they are exhausted, the whole system is positively affected. What one does to the root of the tree is reflected in the trunk, branches, leaves, and fruit.

Mystic visions are quite different from what most people consider "visions." Commonly experienced visions are the stuff of imagination, or the hypnogogic dream-like imagery that arises when brain wave activity reduces to lower alpha (8–12 Hz) and theta (3–8 Hz) states, or mentally formed imaginings from the abstract mind. These are considered inner visions; they are not authentic mystic visions.

The three types of visions are external, which are the images or scenes detected with the gross physical eyes; internal, which are the images and scenes generated by the brain; and authentic mystic visions, which are a unique experience generated in a state between the other two. These three different visual states can also be referred to as outer, inner, and secret visions. For the sake of realization, our method only makes use of the secret or concealed authentic mystic visions.

Gazing practice (vision practice) begins to awaken and arouse dormant very subtle elemental energy and allows access to the lesser-known energy channel connecting the subtle heart and mind. Very subtle habitual tendencies are generated and appear through fine visional anomalies in the space between one's usual external and internal visions; the emergence of intensifying visions indicates the depth of the heart-mind connection.

To arouse authentic mystic visions, the key for success lies in one's ability to keep the body, heart, and mind stable and motionless while remaining relaxed. The physical eyes must also become motionless, with relaxed focus held correctly in the specified position.

Without stillness, it is impossible to generate authentic visions. The space between the perceiver and the perceived, where secret visions arise, contains special concealed information that is missed by the majority of humanity. It appears to be empty of anything interesting or substantial, but the mystic knows better. The same space that seems empty is where the most fascinating opportunities for delving into the unknown reside.

When the senses are left alone, and one keeps the eyes and body motionless, the secrets of the heart-mind connection arise in the form of special signs. These signs (the visions) are generated in different stages depending on how the heart-mind connection has improved (through the secret energy channel) during consecutive practice sessions.

Progression through the vision practices is crucial to the method; they are the core and basis for one's breakthrough into stream-entry. They refine the disturbing very subtle elemental energies while creating the ever-increasing correct view of awareness, allowing the critical heart-mind unification to occur.

When the instructions are followed correctly, the elimination of very subtle elemental energies simultaneously awakens the awareness until dream and deep sleep lucidity emerge on their own. One who has activated the vividly clear and lucid dreaming and deep sleep perception inevitably reveals the field of nonconceptual emptiness. This revelation creates the potential to finalize permanently sealed realization from the union of insight (awakened awareness) and emptiness.

In maintaining the proper gaze, one seeks to become aware of the *in-between* nature of the space that rests neither out in the distance nor within the mind's projections. This gaze rests in the nonconceptual field of emptiness.

The right gaze is kindled over time, becoming more robust with activation of the air element center (heart, touch faculty), the space element center (throat, hearing faculty), and the physical eyes. Never focus on anything specific; the gaze is completely relaxed along with relaxed breath, body, and mind.

There are several ways one can ensure the gaze is correct for the practice. One might establish it by going outside to look up at the sky during the day. Looking up at the open sky with a soft, unfocused gaze reveals a multitude of small undulating lines of light that dart to and fro on the surface of the eyes, appearing somewhere in the space just in front of the eyes. Once this state is noticed and that unfocused gaze can be maintained, that same view can be replicated within any other chosen environment.

One can establish the gaze by extending the arm out with the thumb raised, focusing on the tip of the thumb. Once established, simply drop the thumb out of sight while remaining aware of the in-between, the space in front of the eyes, while opening the awareness so there is no focus on any particular thing. Soften the awareness into the entire field of perception. Gazing can also be practiced using the image at the end of this chapter (figure 3).

The vision practices are highly advanced, and the practitioner must attend to several critical points, either in succession or in combination. For example, as one activates and draws the navel center back while applying special awareness in the heart center coupled with breath retention, the eyes and ears are held open and clear.

The entire step-by-step process must be understood before an attempt is made; get help from an expert teacher to grasp the nuance.

The practices include successful maintenance of:

- *Right posture*: where each posture specifically influences the opening and closing of certain elemental energy channels to help induce refinement and the emergence of the stream-entry gateway.
- *Right view of awareness*: maintaining an ultra-wide focus of the entire periphery of awareness, so that no matter what phenomena rise or fall, they do not disturb one's view of continuous nonconceptual emptiness.
- *Right centers*: holding the air center, space center, and physical eyes in certain ways simultaneously to induce more intense visual states; also drawing the navel area in to raise bliss-warmth upwards to the heart.
- *Right eye position*: where each eye position is related to a specific elemental energy and helps to refine it directly. These gaze directions also relate with the kinds of visions being generated.

With correct application, wonderful images appear. Initial images refine, becoming stable and motionless. These more stable elemental energies invade normal waking visions, where phenomena involving breath, heat, cold, density, and even more elusive phenomena reveal their intrinsic nature through color and light. Visions can appear as circles, spheres, waves, illuminated hologram-like images, threads, strings of gems, or triangles linked in intricate lattice networks with seeds at the connecting points. The body's subtle channels and energy centers are illuminated; the organs, fluids, muscles, tendons, and even the elemental energies become visible. Eventually, the heavenly fields themselves manifest in the vision, bringing one in contact with the intelligent governing forces that exist in the most subtle mind, controlling one's experiences through the body.

Different expressions within the visions relate to the elemental energy connection: white ellipsoid to space, green circle or tetrahedron to air, red triangle to fire, blue semicircle to water, and yellow square to earth. The colors help indicate which element is predominant at the time of the vision.

Visions deepen until a perpetual state of clarity emerges, when the most subtle habitual tendencies have been exhausted. Here, visions still exist, but one is no longer fettered by attachments to them. And with the release of subtle root entanglements, all of the branch level attachments fall away.

Visions become a part of one's every waking minute; the entire physical environment bleeds into waking consciousness. There is no *this and that*, no *you and other*, there is only the continual stream of pure realization of the structure of creation, as it is. Not illusory, but not *not illusory;* a kind of dream-like play of the mind that is being experienced by itself and through others, interdependently connected. This is where fears are completely released and life emerges with new meaning, free to be enjoyed as a wondrous journey that will continue long past the death of the transient body. One finds the truth of reality, seeing phenomena and nonconceptual emptiness just as they are; this is called true sight, or opening the luminous eye of wisdom.

Furthermore, this exhaustion of habitual tendencies creates the perfect environment for one's eventual physical death, where similar experiences arise within the stages of the dying process. With attachments exhausted, one is free to leap over and avoid the chance of being drawn back into the physical realm of cyclical suffering and delusion.

Proper application of visionary practices generates a series of special indicators that signify successful refinement of the elemental energies. These indicators appear in three distinct ways: Through achievement of gradually more intense images within the field of visions, through changes in the dream and deep sleep states, and through changes in one's waking life.

Changes that occur in the field of visions

- In the first stage, one notices temporary and unclear dashing streaks of light that turn into subtle sparks, like fireflies, or bursts of light like the flashes of a tiny camera.
- Subtle visions change and emerge with more detail, including fog, heat-like waves, static, motionless light, wavy flames, and other subtle visual anomalies that become more regular, clear, and intense.
- More stationary shapes with colors start to emerge, shifting depending on posture and eye direction.
- The colored shapes eventually transform into webs of fluctuating interconnected seeds (the size of mustard seeds), garland-like flower arrangements, outflowing fractal knots, and interconnected triangles forming lattice-like mandalas of brilliant color and light.
- Eventually, the connecting-seeds at each joint in the lattice open to expose the heavenly fields, which open up like a scroll that is burning from the middle outward to reveal profound and intense scenes of thrones, castles, landscapes, heavenly beings, and much more.

These visions exhaust the most subtle underlying habitual tendencies, leading to the revelation of pure authentic emptiness prior to stream-entry.

Changes that occur in sleep states

- Regular recall of dream details.
- Discontinuation of negative or bad dreams as the subtle habitual tendencies expire.
- As subtle elemental energies are refined, dream lucidity (dream aware-ness and control) begins on its own.
- Dream projections are eventually exhausted and are replaced with pure deep sleep clear-awareness, preparing one with a firm awareness for the future death process.

Changes that occur in waking life

- Temporal mental, emotional, and physical disturbances may rise up.
- After potential initial increase, mental disturbances decrease.
- After potential initial increase, emotional disturbances decrease.
- After potential initial increase, physical disturbances decrease.

Vision practices bring about profound insights and wonderful visual experiences within the mind's eye, so it is important that the practitioner has already developed stable mental and emotional will. If unprepared, one can easily get caught up in visions and misunderstand them; this leads to chasing desired states or phenomena and being dragged unconsciously into more delusion and egoic confusion. These practices have typically been concealed because of this heightened potential for practitioners to fall into misunderstandings through fallacious assumptions, failing to attain the right insights that would lead to breakthrough. One must sufficiently accomplish the foundational practices for establishing the view and purification of the gross elemental energies beforehand.

And while it is generally safe to speak about one's personal level of attainment along the path of realization, one must keep in mind that speaking about unique or personal experiences arising from those attainments is not helpful to others. The state of nonconceptual stream-realization is beyond definition or explanation of any kind, and one's attempts to express it openly only confuse and create negative impressions for others. Hearing the details of another's mystic visions, dreams, or deep sleep experiences can raise massive barriers in the seeker's subconscious mind, and while the sharing may appear harmless at first, subtle impressions remain and inevitably work against their progress. Remember that whatever visions come to fill one's radiant clarity through this process should be kept personal and private, only shared between teacher and student; this rule should be followed carefully at all times.

figure 3: optional gazing practice image

16

The Practice Area

Misunderstandings and rumors about the purpose and use of the ritual altar have circulated in and around the spiritual community, spreading confusion, superstition, and fear.

In truth, the altar is simply the workspace of the mystic, an important tool that can aid in the process. For one, the altar might be nothing more than a meditation cushion and a prayer shawl. For another, it could contain a myriad of ritual implements such as a *kila* or ritual dagger, a wand, deity statues, incense, oil lamps, bells, offering bowls, and so forth.

In the traditional view, the altar is a place where prayer, devotion, and meditation are performed. It is where communication with the divine is accomplished at varying levels of intensity and sensitivity depending on the mystic's attainment. The practice is a way of connecting intention and giving gratitude toward the All in whatever form or manifestation might appeal to each person.

As sensitivity, competency, and consciousness expand with time and practice, one becomes more aware of the subtle nature of reality, the dimension that transcends limited physical senses. One begins to notice the very delicate waves of subtle phenomena responsible for influencing the physical domain;

and in becoming more aware of the hidden dimension, one comes to know there are a myriad of intelligent governing forces operating there.

The mystic always desires insight, knowledge, and wisdom about the self and the structure of creation. Progressing through the path, one is always trying to expand awareness beyond the confines of the limited tactile senses. When this expansion starts to occur, as the mystic approaches realization, the personal altar can become a place of great help.

As one interacts with the intelligent governing forces in an effort to learn about them and connect with them, the altar becomes an important space for the accumulation and preservation of conducive energies. The implements, offering items, *yidam, yantras*, symbols, and other special sacraments receive and maintain a subtle charge of elemental energies that increases with time. These subtle energies represent an imprint of some aspect of one's being, whether that is made deliberately in the case of advanced mystic applications, or whether that is simply from being handled and in close proximity. Regardless, these items, the altar, and the environment all become unique and personal to the mystic; this is why it is important not to let others invade the space, meditate there, or handle personal altar items.

This unique imprint strengthens and attracts receptive energies to the altar space that allow one to fulfill mystical goals. This is why it is vital to maintain the same kind of energy, the same kind of process, and the same kind of intention each time one sits in the altar area.

The altar area can be created in a small corner of a room, in a closet, at the foot of the bed, or even in the attic. The bubble of space that surrounds and is the altar area simply has to be kept clean of other energies so they do not harm the personal energetic conditions that one has already reinforced. If someone happens to contaminate the items, the area, or any other part of the altar space, it is important to understand how to purify the items and the area again.

Consecration of the altar space, altar items, and the process of purification are explained in the Gift-Blessings Offering practice (chapter 25); these should be done at certain times within the lunar and solar cycles, or when the altar has become potentially contaminated with unwanted outside energies.

The (approximately) 29.5-day lunar cycle has a significant influence on one's personal energies and affects how and when one performs certain kinds of altar operations, meditations, supplications, or rituals. The solar cycle is drawn out over 12 months, but is similar to the lunar cycle in that it also influences certain aspects of the energies surrounding the mystic and the altar. One can think of the lunar cycle as magnetic and the solar cycle as electric. Although these are ultimately the same forces, in the realm of physical duality they perform different duties.

Each lunar day is associated with a lunar house or mansion which represents a specific energetic influence, and these energetic influences are the intelligent governing forces. Each governing force has a specific influence on one's body and the surrounding energies. How these influences are used internally, or externally toward the various altar items, is part of the mystic's *play* within the subtle dimension of creation.

The new moon occurs when the moon is positioned between the earth and sun. Only the far side of the moon (the half that cannot be seen from the earth) is illuminated, so this phase is also referred to as the dark moon.

At the full moon, the earth, the moon, and the sun are in a similar alignment to the new moon phase, but this time, the moon is on the opposite side of the earth, with its entire face illumined by the sun and the dark portion completely hidden from view.

During the first quarter and third quarter moons, referred to as half moons, the moon is positioned to the side of the earth, at a 90 degree angle with respect to its earlier alignment with the earth and sun. One sees half of the moon illuminated and half in shadow. These half moons are also referred to as crescent, gibbous, waxing, and waning. Crescent refers to phases where the moon is less than half illuminated. Gibbous refers to phases where the moon is more than half illuminated. Waxing means the moon is being illuminated more each night as the full moon approaches, while waning means the moon is being illuminated less each night as the new moon approaches.

The moon travels through these four phases of new moon, half moon, full moon, and half moon again, until the cycle restarts. With these four key moon phases understood, one should also understand how the energies of each of these positions, and the positions between them, influence the earth and one's own energies.

It was mentioned that the moon represents the magnetic (lunar) energy. This lunar energy is influenced by the electric (solar) energy of the sun. The various combinations of lunar and solar energetic conditions impact the mystic's internal and external elemental energies and the various practices. When the moon is new, it exhibits the least amount of solar influence; the moon is blocking a portion of the solar energy toward the earth, and this is when the moon's influence is most magnetic in nature. When the moon's illumination starts to grow, it mixes its magnetic force with the sun's solar electric force. When the moon reaches its full stage, the lunar magnetic influence is matched with the sun's solar electric influence; this is a time of brimming energy, as one can see by the way this moon phase influences tides around the world. After the full phase, the moon's solar influence decreases as it returns to more of its lunar aspect, until the new moon is reached with its fully magnetic influence.

Solar and lunar influences are fairly important, and there are four segments of solar (electric) energetic influence. These segments are more commonly known as the four seasons: spring, summer, autumn (fall), and winter. They are also directly related with the four major elements of earth, water, fire,

93

and air. In each of the four seasons or elements, there are three divisions known as growth, life, and decay. Taking the approximate summer season in the northern hemisphere as an example: June is the time the fire grows; it sustains through July, and August is its period of decline or decay as September begins to introduce the growth of the air element. Each of these quarters and their individual subdivisions impact on the kind of lunar energy that is experienced each month. For example, in June, when fire is expanding, each of the lunar days have a solar influence based in the element of fire. This fire-growing quality gives a special flavor to each lunar day it influences. In July, the fire reaches its peak and then withdraws, and this type of fire influence has a unique impact on each lunar day as well. In August, when the fire is decaying and the air is being invited in, the lunar days are still influenced more toward fire, even as it is reduced.

The monthly and yearly energetic impacts also influence one's daily waking and sleeping states in important ways. All of these influences affect each person differently depending on how individual elements rule over one's unique physical and subtle systems. To make a very general and simplistic example, if one has a more fiery nature with a lack of water element, then the summer months will increase this fire and cause a subtle impact on the fire element within, as well as on the fire element outside in the macrocosmic environment. And during the winter months where water is prevalent, the same system will become more even; the person might find a more balanced and relaxed perception during that time. This is how the imprint of energy at the time of birth is influenced by the yearly and monthly cycles, both internally and externally.

Volume II, *The Luminous Eye of Wisdom*, explains another larger cycle, along with methods and practices using solar and lunar forces in combination with elemental qualities to fulfill various mystical operations. It contains practical applications for use of elemental energies to explore and better understand the nature of the physical and subtle realities; these operations help mitigate the internal and external cycles one faces every day.

As more clarity and sensitivity to the surrounding subtle energies is attained, correct use of various cycles of energy affords one pivotal influence on the path, on operations at the altar, and on life in general. Imagine seeking to connect with a certain kind of governing force that has the qualities of water, with a specific combination of rising electric and magnetic energies; one would find that performing an operation in January (winter) during the rising moon would bring the most powerful and precise results.

Once the mystic begins to understand the value and specific quality of each elemental energy, the timing of the various elemental months (in growing, sustaining, or decaying solar functions), along with the combination of lunar and solar energies, the attainment of certain ritual activities is much more certain and can be powerfully precise.

17

Physical Well-Being

One's body can be a great aid or a great barrier on the path. Proper stretching and breathing are essential for maintaining health so the body does not become an unnecessary obstacle, but one does not need to be a fitness or food fanatic; it will not help. Fortunately, the body can be kept pliable, healthy, and full of vigor and spirit through simple practices, done daily or on alternating days depending on age and health.

Everyone has a different blend of elemental energy disturbances and different needs. For a healthy and happy body, one should take a mindful and balanced approach to food, drink, breathing, sleep, and regular exercise. When planning, simply address these important aspects in the most balanced and personally beneficial ways possible. The overall goal is to keep the body very loose, relaxed, and limber to help reduce restrictions and positively influence the elemental energies for more advanced practices in later stages.

For most, a simple stretching routine, a healthy diet, breathing purification practice, and proper rest are essential to the path. Nothing needs to be done in an extreme way. Unfortunately, many people today are already harming themselves through too little movement, too many unhealthy foods, and poor quality rest. An imbalanced lifestyle causes major issues on the path, where one's body is required to be fresh, healthy, and full of vitality.

The good news is that even elders can make simple adjustments to diet and exercise habits that significantly benefit the investigation of the mind. Various types of exercise that work in conjunction with proper diet and rest can be investigated and tailored to one's specific needs.

One powerful and effective pliability practice is the 5 Tibetan rites. Perform 12–21 rounds each (depending on personal experience) for a minimum of 3 days per week to help keep the spine, hips, and neck limber and pliable, and to provide essential adjustments to the elemental energies. Alternatively, one could use the sun salutation yoga postures, or other preferred forms of stretching or energy practice like qigong, tai chi, etc. Any number of other pliability and energy exercises can help loosen and make the body healthy during the course of one's practice. Regardless of what is chosen, some kind of daily or bidiurnal pliability practice is highly encouraged to help relieve many of the elemental energy disturbances on the gross level.

When short on time, the most important considerations are that the hips are opened, the spine and neck are pliable and limber, and the blood is moving; these can be accomplished with a simple after-dinner walk or bike ride, etc.

Drink enough water and eat only when the body is hungry. Eat slowly, and only enough so the body is not completely full; remain slightly hungry, wanting just a little more. Only eat what the body, not the tongue, desires—think about overall health and nutrition, not just pleasure. Be sure to eat a good balance of foods with enough nutrient-rich vegetables, proteins, and carbohydrates that provide what the body needs. Watch the breath throughout the day to make sure it is relaxed and not inhibited, strained, stressed, or unnecessarily shallow in the chest. Let it be natural, but calm, deep, and subtle. Get to sleep relatively early, and wake at the same time each day to help stabilize vital hormone production. Never sleep after eating; always wait 3–5 hours after a meal to sleep, and always try to fall asleep with a positive, happy, and contented outlook.

18

Meditative Postures

Some people think about sitting like the eastern yogis and immediately start to ache—I do not blame them. When I began meditative practice as a child, my teacher forced me to sit in what is known as full lotus posture. He knew that proper sitting and breathing are important aspects of mystical practice.

The term *posture* refers to how one maintains the body during meditative practices. At age 7, it was fairly easy to adjust to the lotus posture, and because I continued throughout my life, it remained easy; with 35 years in martial arts, my body has remained strong and limber. Early in life, I had assumed that everyone's body was like this, and that everyone could easily assume this meditative posture; however, I quickly learned this is not so.

Having taught martial arts to both general practitioners and the highest grade athletes, I can say with confidence that the biggest obstacle to physical ease is lack of pliability in the body. It is extremely difficult for one with limited flexibility to establish valuable meditative postures without experiencing great pain and discomfort. Although this is changing in recent times, many people in western countries are not used to sitting in lotus, full lotus, or similar postures. Some feel these are almost a form of torture, not a comfortable way of relaxing into meditative equipoise or sitting for dinner.

Most westerners were taught to sit in chairs instead of sitting on the ground, and they did not grow up in home environments where seated meditation is common like it is in some eastern cultures. Further, traditional physical practices for total body health and flexibility are more commonly found in the east than the west.

When sitting to investigate the nature of mind, one of the most important factors for getting the body out of the way is comfort. When the spine is straight with the shoulders held comfortably back, chin down, and neck aligned with the hips, the body responds with improved blood circulation, ease in the spine, better nerve connection, increased depth and length of breath, reduced pressure on organ systems, and so forth. In the beginning, the comfort gained from maintaining correct posture can help one explore the inner process and make positive insights there without unnecessary distraction from the body.

This body is going to die and become food for the worms; there is no way to avoid it. So while the current vessel is available, one should take full advantage of it as a vehicle for exploration of the subtle mind. The subtle awareness of mind is what allows one to make corrections to the overall perception of reality. A clear, unfettered perception is of paramount importance for a clean, clear, and meaningful life experience. Keeping the body limber and pliable ensures that it does not present an obstacle during the investigation of the nature of mind. Right posture makes investigation easier, and for ease in sitting, it is important that the physical body is healthy, or is at least getting healthier along the way.

Volumes of text have been written about the importance of posture, not just in the yogic (asana) community, but in the medical and athletic communities as well. It is easy to see that the posture one holds places pressure on or removes pressure from the physical body and its subtle system; changes in the posture can impact one's health and energy.

Meditative sitting is not just about being still while engaged in meditative practice, it is also about the specific postures one holds and how these influence the subtle elemental energies. The way one holds the body, like an asana (posture) in hatha yoga, either enhances or corrupts the inner wind energies. Over time, continually imbalanced posture influences some or all of the subtle winds in a negative way, and this works against one's ability to achieve suppleness and overall health in body and mind.

As sensitivity to the subtle energies within the body increases, one can more easily discern how even the most subtle adjustments to some aspect of the posture or breath can affect entry into the deepest states of awareness. When the body is not a hindrance and can be let go of, one enters into deep investigation easily and efficiently.

A wide variety of seated postures can be applied for one's advancement toward realization. One could sit upright in a chair and use only the most basic meditative practices to gain great benefits like improved focus, a calmer mind, better emotional stability, etc. But when it comes to working with the very subtle energies, the mystic knows that the body can also be used as a tool to help cut off certain energy channels while keeping others open, enhancing energy flow and influence for specific purposes.

It is important to perform gentle stretching several times per week to open the hips, stretch the spine, and generally keep the elemental energies flowing seamlessly. A few simple practices to improve pliability and energy flow are introduced for this purpose in Physical Well-Being (chapter 17).

In the beginning, just use the most comfortable and manageable posture, keeping the neck, spine, and hips in alignment to avoid causing unnecessary bad habits or energy disorders. It is important not to slouch, and to ensure the neck is comfortably straight with the chin drawn slightly down to extend the neck and spine.

Overall body position, including sitting with a straight spine, tilting the neck, staying taut, drawing the shoulders back, and holding the hands in specific ways (known as *mudras)*, will adjust and correct subtle energies while one is learning to attain and deepen emptiness (will) and insight (intention).

The specific position of the legs impacts one's downward or earth energy. The earth elemental energy influences the health of the physical body.

The hands being pressed to the body and held in specific ways influences the contracting energy of the water element, which in turn directly influences the balance or imbalance of one's emotional desires.

Holding the spine straight and the body taut helps control one's expanding energies related to the air element, which influences mental conditions (agitation, balance, or dullness).

The position of the arms helps control the upward fire element, which is directly related to the energies of intention.

Bending the neck to a certain angle, resting the eyes in a certain position, and naturally touching the tongue to the palate are ways to control the surrounding energies of the space element, which impact the strength of awareness itself.

Even the tilt of one's posture influences the subtle elemental energies. For example, leaning right brings clarity faster, but bliss suffers because one eventual clings to the objects of form (phenomena). Leaning left brings bliss faster, but clarity decreases when one eventually clings to the subject (self). Leaning forward brings initial clarity, but later agitation. Leaning back brings initial calm, but eventually dullness.

One's gaze can have a powerful influence on the subtle energies of mentation and awareness. The mystic vision states described in this method, which allow one to eliminate very subtle elemental energy disorders, require the maintenance of postures and gazes in combination to help energies flow correctly during the various applications.

Holding any meditative posture in relaxed stillness can allow the elemental energies of the body to also become stilled. When the energies are still, they have the ability to blend back together in a state of serenity called entering the central channel. This serene stillness allows the awareness to direct its focus and energy to the desired destination with less interference and interruption.

The longer energy is directed toward an object of focus without hindrance, the more arousal is generated there. Most practitioners seeking to arouse or lure elemental energy fail to understand this crucial point. In practice sessions, one must learn to remain as motionless as possible, calming the breath and body, with the awareness remaining on the anchor; this helps to refine gross and subtle elemental energies.

As one progresses along the path, good meditative posture becomes more important, regardless if it is for realization or for any of the ancillary practices discussed in other volumes of this series. For now, it is enough to gain a general overview of the correct way to sit in meditative sessions for maximum overall health, benefit, and comfort.

The postures listed below can be used for the meditative, visionary, and sleep practices. Feel free to start with any of the main or alternative seated postures indicated here as needed. Being uncomfortable is not helpful for relaxation and will make it more challenging to enter the deepest mental and energetic states required for the method to be useful, so choose something that works for now, while the body gets more flexible with advancement through the method. For clarification and further instruction on the practices associated with these postures, be sure to attend the respective lectures at the Drukama Treasury.

Seated and Sleeping Meditative Postures

1. Full Meditative Posture
2. Half Meditative Posture
3. Easy Meditative Posture
4. Alternative Posture
5. Sleep Posture
6. Mystic Vision Postures

The *full meditative posture*, also known as *padmasana*, is a cross-legged seated meditation pose where each foot is placed up on the opposite thigh. This is the most stable, energetically effective, and important posture of them all. The problem with this posture is that most are not flexible enough to use it effectively. One should never force the body into this posture as it can cause damage to the knees and joints. Only use this posture if it comes easily, without strain or tension.

The *half meditative posture*, also known as *ardha padmasana*, is with one leg bent and resting on the ground, and the other leg bent with the foot resting on the opposite thigh; the calves are comfortably stacked. It is an easier meditation posture than the full posture and is quite effective.

The *easy meditative posture*, also known as *vajrasana*, is sitting from a kneeling position; the knees are bent and feet are underneath the buttocks. As an alternative, it can be easier on the legs to place a rolled towel or blanket under the thighs or buttocks to help provide support.

The *alternative posture* is sitting on a zazen bench or low meditation chair to keep the body stable, comfortable, and in the correct posture. There are many seats to choose from in the marketplace. With the back, hips, neck, and head remaining straight, comfortable, stable, and firmly established, the posture will work. As long as the legs are not straight, and instead the knees are bent in some way, it can be an effective basic posture for the method.

The *sleep posture* (for dream and deep sleep practice) is used mainly during Preliminary Dream Projection (chapter 37). Sit 45 degrees upright against pillows or some other sturdy support so that the back, neck, and head are aligned; do not lie down completely, and be careful not to lean to the right or the left. One leg is out straight, and the other is bent so that the foot (heel, ideally) is touching, or is close to, the knee of the opposite leg. The hands are either crossed on the chest or down at the sides with the palms facing toward the sky or ceiling. This is one of the most comfortable postures, but it is typically only used for meditative work while sleeping.

In the beginning, lying all the way back (flat) for dream and deep sleep practice can reduce one's chances for dreaming awareness, and the hand position can affect dream clarity. Later, wakeful dreaming will occur regardless of body position.

Five additional postures are used during the mystic vision practices. Each posture influences one specific elemental energy over the rest.

Mystic Vision Postures

In the *earth posture* (figure 4), sit with the buttocks on the floor, feet together and knees to the chest. The arms can wrap around the knees, or can rest on top of the knees so that the forearms raise up and the hands can support the head with fingers resting naturally around the ears. The head remains straight, the back and neck as straight as comfortably possible, and the eyes look gently to the right.

In the *water posture* (figure 5), sit in a comfortable crouching position with the balls of the feet planted on the ground; or, as an alternative, plant the feet flat. To secure the posture, the arms wrap around the knees to support the legs, while the hands hold the opposite wrists or forearms. The head remains straight, the back and neck as straight as comfortably possible, and the eyes look gently downward.

In the *fire posture* (figure 6), sit with the buttocks on the floor, legs opening outward in a butterfly position so the soles of the feet touch each other; with the sides of the feet on the ground and closer to the body. The hands are posted straight behind the body on the ground as support. Make sure a fist could not pass through the space between the underarms and the torso; this ensures the arms and body are close enough to each other. The head remains straight, the back and neck as straight as comfortably possible, and the eyes look gently upward.

In the *air posture* (figure 7), lie down on the right side. The right elbow bends so that the hand is up to cradle the head for support, while the left hand rests on the left thigh comfortably. The calves lay on one another with the knees slightly drawn up and bent in a natural v-shape—the hips and legs can be in any position, as long as the knees are bent. The head remains generally straight (relative to support by the hand), the back and neck as straight as comfortably possible, and the eyes look gently to the left.

In the *space posture* (figure 8), kneel all the way down and bend forward with the head over the knees. The knees are completely bent with the hips drawn back over the feet, and the belly is resting against the knees. The elbows are on the ground in front of the body and the hands rise up to cradle the head for support. The tops of the feet remain down on the ground, providing easy support for the hips and legs. The head faces forward, the rest of the back as straight as comfortably possible, and the eyes remain gently looking straight ahead.

figure 4: earth vision posture

figure 5: water vision posture

figure 6: fire vision posture

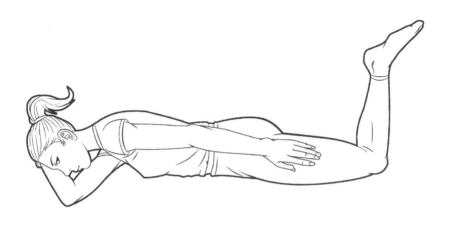

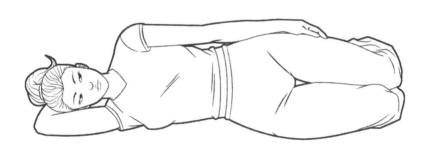

figure 7: air vision posture

figure 8: space vision posture

19

Breathing Techniques

The average person completes a full breath about 20,000 times over 24 hours; however, traditional knowledge about the breath has largely been forgotten. For years, I have reiterated the importance of breath and how it can be used consciously for growth, or unconsciously for decay. The way the breath is being influenced (consciously or unconsciously) causes changes in one's physiological structure according to the underlying energetic conditions.

Breath, food, water, and sleep directly affect the subtle energies of the body. Correct breathing is known to alter health, cure disease, purify energies, stabilize emotions, and settle the mindstream. Respiration is a complex process affecting all parts of the body, and the oxygen intake returns waste from the cells in the form of carbon dioxide. Stale air that was not fully exhaled can remain in the lungs for a long period, so breathing purification practices are important for one's health and path.

The three main parts of breathing can be referred to as inhalation, exhalation, and retention (holding). It is possible to alter the way one feels by using the breath, influencing the three subtle channels of energy (the lunar, solar, and central channels) through adjustments to the speed of the breath, the depth of the breath, and other subtle variances between inhalation and exhalation.

The lunar channel relates to the parasympathetic nervous system, the rest and digest cycle; when aroused, it represses excitation and creates relaxation, suppleness, and ease. The solar channel relates to the sympathetic nervous system, the fight or flight cycle; when stimulated, it creates excitation, action, movement, and arousal. The central channel is aroused when the lunar and solar channels flow back and forth between each other. When the solar channel is active, the right nostril flows with slightly more air than the left. When the lunar channel is active, the left nostril flows with slightly more air than the right. When the central channel is active, both flow equally.

When purified, the solar is considered the channel of bliss, and the lunar is considered the channel of clarity. Together, they combine within the central channel to form nondual bliss-clarity, the state of stream-entry.

In a healthy person, the solar and lunar channels sway into each other about every 72 minutes. The body cycles through the channels regularly, day and night, and airflow in the respective nostrils changes accordingly. These cycles are also influenced by the cycles of nature and the seasons, and are directly related to the activities of the sun, the moon, the planets, and the time of day; all of these factors influence one's physical and mental conditions.

The cycle also relates to the activity of the pervading elemental energy. The active elemental energy within the left and right channels, the lunar and solar channels, dictates how one is influenced to a more subtle degree. Noticing the length of the breath is one way to investigate this phenomena further, as this relates to the elemental influence on each channel.

Understanding the breath, one can generate states consciously to overcome mental activity or passivity, emotional imbalances, and overly sensual states of physical desire.

The nasal passages act as filter, thermostat, and humidifier for the air that travels into the body. This is why it is important to breathe through the nose when entering into deep meditative states. Breathing through the nose also influences the very subtle energies that flow into the body, helping to drive that energy to specific areas of concentration; this information is explored in more detail in the next volume of this series.

If the exhalation of the left nostril is long and can be felt or sensed on a mirror 18 inches away from the nostril, this means that lunar earth is predominate. Lunar earth is a grounded state that seeks to withdraw, usually the kind of breath that makes one sleepy or very relaxed. If the exhalation of the right nostril is short and can be faintly felt coming out of the nostril at 2–4 inches, it means that solar air is active. The solar air breath would indicate a very active mental state, where the mind is engaged in thinking and intellectual operations, even over-excitation. Elemental qualities are discussed in more detail in Chapter 11.

During the normal breathing cycle, each phase of the breath influences a different element. As the breath draws in during inhalation, energy rises up to influence the fire element. Near the end of the inhalation, energy expands outward, influencing the expanding air element. The slight pause at the top of the inhalation influences space, the vastness of the area of play. On release of the breath in the exhalation, energy falls downward to influence the water element. Near the end of the exhalation, energy condenses to influence earth energy. In the pause at the end of the exhalation, the space element is influenced once again.

The natural process of breathing balances one's elemental energies as it helps cycle through the physiological influences. Each element has its own unique quality related to one's sense-desires and emotional, mental, and intuitive faculties. Each element is not distinct or separate from the other; they blur into each other through their sub-elements. The entire play of the breath and the elements can be seen if one is diligent with conscious clarity toward the interaction of the breath and the faculties of the identity-body.

For example, while the breath is being condensed down into the earth cycle, one is never thinking about problems or solutions. When one thinks, the breath is very subtle. It draws up toward fire and air, and may even be automatically retained to increase the space element while one waits for a connection to that higher akashic-like area to open and reveal the answer.

In a state of anger, one's breath is focused on exhalation and the density of the earth element, while being inhaled to fill the belly and chest; this is where the expression *all puffed up* is applied, when describing an arrogant or haughty person.

When one feels depressed or down, rather than the breath concentrating in that higher inhaled state, it is more concentrated in the exhalation, near the water and the earth elements. This is where the term *deflated* comes from, when speaking about someone who has given up, or is feeling down.

When someone has a habit such as shallow breathing, chest breathing, or depressed breathing, all kinds of mental, emotional, and physical aliments occur. Bad breathing habits are prevalent with drug use, where the system is forced to breathe in very unnatural ways, resulting in emotional distance, mental overactivity, paranoia, sleeplessness, premature aging, and all kinds of other acute ailments which can arise very quickly in the overall system.

Through just these few examples, one can see the intimite relationship betweenthe breath and the elemental energies and how they work together. Breath is such a vast subject; the full science of breathing and elemental energy cannot be covered within the scope of this manual. For those who are interested in exploring further, this topic and many others are discussed in much more detail in Volume II and at the Drukama Treasury.

For the mystic, the breath is an important instrument that allows one to create, enter different states of consciousness, adjust energies, and influence the way reality is perceived. One first makes use of the breath to adjust the overall system, in order to break away from the physiologically created habitual tendencies that drive the personality in harmful ways toward oneself and others. Later, the breath is used in a much more advanced way to influence the outward (solar) and inward (lunar) aspects of the elements so that one can interfere with and play with the structure of creation itself.

II

PRACTICE

Practical basis for achievement of stream-realization and exploration of the subtle dimensions of reality.

These teachings are complemented by ongoing lectures and discussions at the Drukama Treasury.

20

Preliminary Meditation

Practical applications build on the theoretical information in Part I. For clarification and further instruction on this and subsequent practices, be sure to attend the respective lectures at the Drukama Treasury.

* * *

T his practice relaxes the body and generates a bit of energy movement while simultaneously preparing the meditative awareness and reducing gross elemental energy disturbances.

It is the first of many practices, and it is the key to establishing a solid foundation for everything that follows. Take whatever time is needed with it to help solidify meditative strength and fortitude; without these qualities, future practice will be impotent.

During this meditation and in all future practices, remember to develop and maintain the right view while also remaining mindful of straying. Make use of resistance breath with focus in the belly combined with the tools of tightening and loosening to help restore the view and re-focus on the anchor whenever it is lost, or to help relax if any strain or tension builds.

Additional References

- Theory, chapter 12: The Right View
- Theory, chapter 13: Adjusting Single-Pointed Focus
- Theory, chapter 18: Meditative Postures
- Theory, chapter 19: Breathing Techniques

Preliminary Meditation Practice

1. Establish a comfortable meditative posture.
2. The eyes can be positioned naturally and allowed to close gently without any coercion, or they can remain open if this feels more comfortable.
3. Place the thumb of each hand at the base of the ring finger. Collapse the fingers around the thumbs in the form of a fist. The fists lie comfortably on the upper thighs, palm side facing upward toward the sky.
4. Generate a state of meditative equipoise using resistance breathing (ocean breathing) to ensure the breath is restrained, even, long, slow, and rhythmic. Continue this deep, natural, and gentle belly breath for several moments to relax the mind and body.
5. As breathing settles into the periphery of the awareness, let go of that focus by devaluing it; let the breath become unnoticeably natural.
6. However the eyes have settled, let go of the seeing faculty, what the eyes are noticing internally or externally. Let the faculty of seeing become unimportant and uninteresting, disregarding it more and more. The awareness is free to move from anchor to anchor through this session.
7. Gently shift the awareness from sensing the breath to sensing the anchor at the bridge of the nose, near the lower inside corners of both eyes. Just rest at this anchor in single-pointed focus without seeking, expecting, or wondering about what is coming next. Let go, relax the entire body, and generate a sense of contentment so that the only focus is the feeling/sensing at the anchor. All forms of conceptualization or discrimination of the mind are allowed to drop away into the background and remain unimportant. Let the mindstream and the body

do what they want; simply ignore them through gentle reminders that they have no value at this time. Only the anchor should be felt/sensed while everything else falls to the periphery of awareness.

8. While steadying the awareness and settling into the anchor, notice and sense any energy that might be there as well. Further establish the anchor by continually feeling/sensing there for a few minutes.

9. When ready, slowly move the awareness from the bridge of the nose near the eyes to the area just below the nostrils, on the upper lip. Feel and sense subtle energy, or just air flowing in and out, at this anchor for a few moments to establish continual single-pointed focus there.

10. When ready, slowly and gently move the awareness from below the nostrils down into the root of the tongue within the throat. Rest in the sensation and feeling at this new anchor continuously without straying.

11. After establishing a stable seal between the awareness and the anchor point at the root of the tongue in the throat, contemplate: "What is sensing the anchor?" Contemplating this question allows the awareness to attempt to perceive (sense/feel) the vantage point of the perceiver by gently letting go of the perceived anchor and searching for the aspect that perceives—what is noticing the anchor? This contemplation may last only a moment, or it may last longer; time is not important for now.

12. After trying to become aware of the perceiver for a few moments, return to the anchor at the root of the tongue (step 10), feeling and sensing.

13. Continue to move the awareness between the perceived anchor at the root of the tongue (step 10) and the perceiver of the anchor (step 11) a few more times before ending the meditation session. It is alright if no "answers" come from the contemplation, the mere attempt is already helping awaken awareness of the field of perception.

14. When ready, finish the session by taking a few deep breaths, similar to what was done at the beginning of the practice, but this time with the eyes looking gently upward toward the sky.

Keep going with these practice sessions until consistent and effortless continuity of concentration on the object of investigation is established and awareness settles easily into the meditation each time. This could take a week for experienced meditators, or it could take months for those with little meditative experience. Most importantly, take all the time that is needed, only moving on to the next practice when proficiency in this basic process has been achieved.

These sessions should last 20–30 minutes. Continue the practice each day at sunrise or sunset, or at night before 10:30 pm. When straying only occurs once or twice per practice, it is time to move on.

21

Energy Purification

This breathing practice helps stabilize the subtle energies, balance the emotions, and calm mental abstractions to bring about more ease in the overall practice process.

Additional References

- Theory, chapter 11: Elements, Channels, and Centers
- Theory, chapter 13: Adjusting Single-Pointed Focus
- Theory, chapter 18: Meditative Postures
- Theory, chapter 19: Breathing Techniques

For this practice, visualize the three main channels of light in the body: white right channel, blue central channel (between both side channels), and red left channel. These channels run through the core of the body just in front of the spine; they flow from the nostrils, around the crown of the head, and down into the body to behind the navel area in the lower belly.

Energy Purification Practice

1. Establish a comfortable meditative posture.
2. The eyes can be positioned naturally and allowed to close gently without

any coercion, or they can remain open if this feels more comfortable.

3. Place the thumb of each hand at the base of the ring finger. Collapse the fingers around the thumbs in the form of a fist. The fists lie comfortably on the upper thighs, palm side facing upward toward the sky.

4. Generate a state of meditative equipoise using resistance breathing (ocean breathing) to ensure the breath is restrained, even, long, slow, and rhythmic. Continue this deep, natural, and gentle belly breath for several moments to relax the mind and body.

5. Gently press the outside ridge of the left hand flush against the side of the left nostril to block airflow and cover the left eye.

6. While slowly and deeply inhaling, visualize a small white ball that travels with the breath; use this to sense the breath as it follows the white solar path, flowing in through the nostril, over the skull, and down through the right side of the body adjacent to the central channel, down into the lower belly.

7. Gently and comfortably retain the breath in the lower belly for a few moments while switching hands from left to right.

8. Gently press the outside ridge of the right hand flush against the side of the right nostril to block airflow and cover the right eye.

9. Following the pathway of the red left channel, exhale slowly and gently at first, and a bit more forcefully at the end of the exhalation. Visualize the white ball that travels with the breath while sensing the airflow escaping the body.

10. Repeat this part of the exercise (from step 5) for a total of 3 times, retaining the breath gently while switching hands and sensing the increasing openness in the white right channel.

11. For the next round, start with the outside ridge of the right hand flush against the side of the right nostril, covering the right eye.

12. While slowly and deeply inhaling, visualize a small red ball that travels with the breath; use this to sense the breath as it follows the red lunar path, flowing in through the nostril, over the skull, and down through the left side of the body adjacent to the central channel, down into the lower belly.

13. Gently and comfortably retain the breath in the lower belly for a few moments while switching hands from right to left.

14. Following the pathway of the white right channel, exhale slowly and gently at first, and a bit more forcefully at the end of the exhalation. Visualize the red ball that travels with the breath while sensing the airflow escaping the body.

15. Repeat this part of the exercise (from step 11) for a total of 3 times, retaining the breath gently while switching hands and sensing the increasing openness in the red left channel.

16. For the next round, start by slowly and deeply inhaling through both nostrils, visualizing or sensing the breath as it follows both channels, flowing in through the nostrils, over the skull, and down the light blue central channel, down into the lower belly.

17. Gently and comfortably retain the breath within the lower belly for a few moments.

18. Following the pathway of the blue central channel, exhale slowly and gently at first; and at the end of the exhalation, pull slightly inward with the diaphragm and breathe out a bit more forcefully. Visualize or sense any energies of self-doubt and lack of confidence travel out through the crown of the head with the exhale, where they instantly dissolve into the space above the body.

19. Repeat this part of the exercise (from step 16) for a total of 3 times, sensing the increasing openness in the blue central channel.

20. After all rounds are completed, relax and breathe gently and naturally for a few moments to conclude.

Perform this purification breathing early in the morning around sunrise, or later in the day around sunset. Start no later than 9pm; this practice causes increased energy for some, which makes sleep unnecessarily difficult.

Repeat this process daily for at least 21 days to purify, balance, and prepare the energy system for future practice.

22

Elemental Cultivation

This practice helps one become more aware of the subtle elemental energies within the body through sensing the flow of the breath.

From this point forward, through the remainder of the method, one should maintain the sexual and physical desire-energies, the emotional energies, and the mental energies in a tranquil, undisturbed, unstirred, and reserved state.

The right view should also be returned to and held as often as possible. The cultivation and refinement of one's subtle energy is vital during this phase to build the necessary balance and strength of vitality that induces visionary states in later practices.

Additional References

- Theory, chapter 11: Elements, Channels, and Centers
- Theory, chapter 12: The Right View
- Theory, chapter 13: Adjusting Single-Pointed Focus
- Theory, chapter 18: Meditative Postures
- Theory, chapter 19: Breathing Techniques

Elemental Cultivation Practice

The circulation should be allowed to flow on its own, not coerced by sensation or awareness; just notice how the elemental energies work in opposition to the breath. Over time, the process becomes more obvious and substantial. There should be no expectation, only absolute calm abiding while sensing the movement. It takes time to become aware of the subtle function of the elements, so be patient.

1. Establish a comfortable meditative posture.
2. The eyes can be positioned naturally and allowed to close gently without any coercion, or they can remain open if this feels more comfortable.
3. Place the hands one on top of the other like a bowl facing the sky, fingers toward the opposite wrists and thumbs gently touching.
4. Generate a state of meditative equipoise using resistance breathing (ocean breathing) to ensure the breath is restrained, even, long, slow, and rhythmic. Continue this deep, natural, and gentle belly breath for several moments to relax the mind and body.
5. While inhaling, sense the fire element ascending from the lower belly toward the top of the head. In the first part of the inhalation, the fire element rises up, and in the second part of the inhalation, the air element spreads out. While retaining the breath momentarily at the end of the inhalation, the space element remains vast and still.
6. While exhaling, sense the water element descending from the head toward the lower belly. In the first part of the exhalation, the water element falls downward, and in the second part of the exhalation, the earth element condenses. While retaining the breath momentarily at the end of the inhalation, the space element remains vast and still.
7. Repeat from step 5.
8. Relax and breathe gently and naturally for a few moments to conclude.

Continue daily for at least 25–30 minutes. Once the rising, expanding, stilling, falling, and condensing can be perceived, move to the next practice.

23

Clarification of Branches

Thisis waking practice helps one become more aware of the branches of the identity-body: physical, emotional, mental, and perception. Clear identification of the various branches of the identity-body is vital before moving on to the more advanced practices ahead.

Additional Reference

- Theory, chapter 13: Adjusting Single-Pointed Focus

Clarification of Branches Practice

1. Use one of the senses to anchor to an object of investigation. This could be looking at a picture, hearing music, smelling food being cooked, etc.
2. Notice how the sense-desire is attracted or averse to the object of investigation, whether the object is perceived as positive or negative.
3. Make a subtle distinction between the sense faculty and the emotional faculty. How is the emotional resonance different, in any way, from the sense-desire itself? How does the object of investigation feel within?
4. Make a subtle distinction between the emotional feeling and any mentation that is activated toward the object of investigation. Is there thinking, analysis, judgement, conjecture, assumption, conceptual-

ization, etc.? Notice how mentation is different in nature from the emotional energy.

5. Notice how overall perception is happening behind each of the faculties—how the cognition is aware of the mentation, the emotion, and the physical sense-desire all at once. Stay with this for just a moment.

6. When finished noticing the final step of perception, simply return to the usual waking agenda.

This process should be done at least a couple of times per day. Make as many attempts as it takes to come to a point of efficiently moving from one branch to another, fluidly and without much trouble. Once the seamless and clearly segregated perception of each branch is automatic and fluid, continue on to the next practice section.

24

Preparing the Central Channel

This practice prepares the central channel to move and unify elemental energies later in the method. One makes use of subtle breath, visualization, and very gentle, subtle body contractions at the navel, the abdominal walls, and the perineum area.

For this practice, visualize a long, light blue tube, 1 inch in diameter, starting from the crown of the head, running down through the center of the body in front of the spine, and ending behind the navel, where it opens up like a bell or trumpet.

The contractions at the navel, abdominal walls, and perineum require only the gentlest muscular engagement, only what is needed to subtly draw the navel back to create very delicate pressure; be careful not to overdo this or use unnecessary muscles in the contraction stages.

Additional References

- Theory, chapter 11: Elements, Channels, and Centers
- Theory, chapter 13: Adjusting Single-Pointed Focus
- Theory, chapter 18: Meditative Postures
- Theory, chapter 19: Breathing Techniques

Bell Breathing Practice to Prepare the Central Channel

1. Establish a comfortable meditative posture.
2. The eyes can be positioned naturally and allowed to close gently without any coercion, or they can remain open if this feels more comfortable.
3. Place the thumb of each hand at the base of the ring finger. Collapse the fingers around the thumbs in the form of a fist. The fists lie comfortably on the upper thighs, palm side facing upward toward the sky.
4. Generate a state of meditative equipoise using resistance breathing (ocean breathing) to ensure the breath is restrained, even, long, slow, and rhythmic. Continue this deep, natural, and gentle belly breath for several moments to relax the mind and body.
5. However the eyes have settled, let go of the seeing faculty. What is seen is not valued; it is seen through and only rests in the periphery. The awareness is free to sense the breath and elemental energies.
6. Visualize the blue tube running from the crown of the head down to the navel level in front of the spine. The end of the tube opens into a bell facing downward toward perineum.
7. Inhale while slowly and very gently drawing the navel toward the spine to create only the most delicate pressure without unnecessary muscle contraction. While inhaling and drawing the navel back like a bow, slowly and gently draw the perineum up toward the bell of the channel opening. The objective is to gain a more powerful sense of the ascending fire element during this inhalation, over time.
8. When inhalation is complete, with the navel still drawn back and perineum lifted, retain the breath for a comfortable time without strain or stress. This retention should eventually last 25 seconds or longer.
9. Exhale through the nostrils while releasing the navel from the spine and allowing the perineum to lower back into place.
10. Take a few rhythmic, natural deep breaths and repeat from step 7.
11. Relax and breathe gently and naturally for a few moments to conclude.

Practice this daily for 20–30 minutes, moving on after 90 days.

25

Gift-Blessings Offering

D evotion is included in most mystical and spiritual traditions throughout the world, and is an important type of practice. It helps sweeten the seeker, opening the heart and providing gift-blessings which help to support one on the path.

Even if one is an atheist or agnostic, the fact remains that all seekers eventually come to know that other beings exist, both in the physical and beyond it. Some of those subtle beings can be of great benefit on the path, and some are essential to the journey. To receive the necessary help, one can look to the subtle governing forces. One should also go to the teacher for gift-blessings in the form of direct one-on-one interactions and subtle interactions.

Whether one finds devotional affinity toward God (or gods), mother nature, the planets, one's teacher, the group, other historical masters, or the intelligent space that occupies the All, prayer and devotion benefit any serious mystical endeavor. And devoting oneself to the benefit of others, through one's own evolution, is the highest aspiration one can strive for.

One's personal practice area might include a variety of items, such as a meditation cushion (or bench, or chair); a small table or altar space; a devotional piece on the table such as a deity, yantra, book, image, etc.; as well as fresh flower(s), water bowl, oil lamp, incense holder, small bell or drum, prayer shawl, and any other desired implements.

It is important to consecrate the practice space each week, or at least during each new and full lunar cycle. Consecration is in addition to one's daily personal practice, which should include some of the actions below. Use whatever implements are preferred and whatever prayers are found worthy to help increase gift-blessings. Gift-blessings are the grace given from the sentient beings in the unseen that wish to protect and help one overcome obstacles and barriers.

The following sample can be used to as a starting point for customizing one's personal devotional practice in the way that feels most comfortable and natural. There are additional and more advanced or extreme ways to consecrate the practice area; what is offered below is a simple version to begin with.

Additional References

- Theory, chapter 13: Adjusting Single-Pointed Focus
- Theory, chapter 16: The Practice Area

Materials

- Copper bowls, plates, etc. are best for holding offerings (including the lamp and incense), but earthenware may be used as an alternative
- Ghee lamp or vegetable oil lamp
- Incense such as dragon's blood, sage and frankincense, myrrh, sandal-wood, etc
- Pure (blessed) water, distilled if possible
- Small bell, drum, or other natural sound-making device to indicate the beginning and ending each time the practice area is used

- Sacred ash
- Flower(s)
- Any other offerings (such as salt or herbs, sacred scrolls, prayers, etc.) or ritual implements one wishes to include

Preparation

- Fast from food for at least 4–8 hours before consecrating the space
- Consecrate the space any time before 9am or after 4pm, up until 10pm
- Avoid unnecessary talking in the practice area; silence is advised unless chanting or praying
- Cleanse the body in a cool bath or shower before sitting in the devotional space

Consecration of the Practice Space with Gift-Blessings Offerings

1. Light the ghee lamp or vegetable oil lamp and take a fire bath at least on the hands and face.
2. Suffumigate the space with incense.
3. Use sacred ash on the throat, heart, brow center, and hands as preferred.
4. Place into the practice area any important ritual items or items to be blessed.
5. Place the copper (or earthen) water bowl filled with pure water.
6. Ring the small bell or tap the drum to begin.
7. **Simple consecration:** With equal time, focus on each of the main energy centers from the root through the throat center for a couple of minutes (or longer), in succession. While maintaining awareness at each center for those few moments, leave the eyes slightly open, focusing the open vision on the practice space, allowing each elemental center to purify the space through the mind's eye at the brow and the physical eyes.
8. Whisper or mentally recite a prayer or chant offering, or perform a silent meditative intention or a practice.

9. Once the right intention has been established, take a flower petal in the hand and vibrate a vowel sound into it.

10. Place the flower petal into the water offering bowl. This vowel vibration which is being given to the flower, and subsequently to the water in the bowl, should contain intention.

11. Give other offerings, if any, at this time.

12. Ring the small bell or tap the drum to conclude.

13. Once complete, if preferred, cover the space, the offerings, and the water (it is ok to extinguish the lamp and incense; never leave anything burning unattended).

14. Clean up the practice area to help keep the energy clean while away.

A clean body, heart, and mind in conjunction with a clean practice area can give one special gift-blessings that assist with practice attainments. It is important to keep the space ritually pure. Protect it from mundane matters and from other people using or examining this personal practice area (children excluded).

26

Refining Space

This practice helps one refine the very subtle disturbances related to the element of space. These refinement practices help prepare the body and the mind for several important future practices in vision, dream, and deep sleep states.

The seamless resting of one's awareness on the sense faculty with perpetual balance, in the middle and without stress or sluggishness, reduces brainwave activity. This helps calm the body and the mind while simultaneously decreasing the tendencies for unconscious habitual clinging to the sense itself.

As the awareness awakens and the elements are refined, fewer distractions are formed. The awareness is less and less likely to be deluded by and act on transient phenomena.

Additional References

- Theory, chapter 11: Elements, Channels, and Centers
- Theory, chapter 13: Adjusting Single-Pointed Focus
- Theory, chapter 18: Meditative Postures
- Theory, chapter 19: Breathing Techniques

Refining Space Practice

To recover lost focus on the hearing faculty, rest the awareness on the initial anchor to re-establish continuity, then return to the hearing faculty. In time, success with entering the emptiness of hearing itself will improve; be patient.

1. Establish a comfortable meditative posture.
2. The eyes can be positioned naturally and allowed to close gently without any coercion, or they can remain open if this feels more comfortable.
3. Place the thumb of each hand at the base of the ring finger. Collapse the fingers around the thumbs in the form of a fist. The fists lie comfortably on the upper thighs, palm side facing upward toward the sky.
4. Generate a state of meditative equipoise using resistance breathing (ocean breathing) to ensure the breath is restrained, even, long, slow, and rhythmic. Continue this deep, natural, and gentle belly breath for several moments to relax the mind and body.
5. Choose an object as the initial temporary hearing anchor. This can be the silence itself, tinnitus (subtle ringing) in the ears, the room hum, a white noise machine, the sound of nature, waves crashing, a fan motor, instrumental music that is continuous and generic, a small bell, a drum, recorded chanting; any sound the hearing faculty can be anchored on. Use the anchor to stabilize in the initial portion of the practice, and to re-anchor whenever straying from the object of investigation (the hearing faculty) is noticed.
6. After focusing gently on the initial anchor, draw the awareness back from the anchor and bring it to the nonconceptual sense faculty itself. Let the original anchor blend into the periphery, into the background of the perception, by perceiving *through* it and instead resting the awareness on the sense faculty itself.
7. Once a consistent anchor of awareness on the sense faculty has been established, contemplate the notion: "What is hearing?" Allow the awareness to investigate the nature of the sense faculty itself, which is always active, letting go of what is being heard by the hearing process;

this will help settle the awareness into the sense faculty.

8. Remain in this single-pointed focus with investigative intention on the nonconceptual faculty of hearing as much as possible without straying.

9. Relax and breathe gently and naturally for a few moments to conclude.

Perform this practice for 20–40 minutes each morning during sunrise or in the afternoon during sunset. If these times are not conducive because of lifestyle, the practice can be performed at night, any time before 11:30 pm.

It is important to keep an approximate record of the amount of straying in each session to compare over the weeks. Move on when straying only occurs 1–2 times total per session for several sessions in a row.

27

Refining Fire

This practice helps one refine the very subtle disturbances related to the element of fire and the sense of sight. Remember to rest awareness on the sense faculty with perpetual balance, in the middle, without coercion, stress, or sluggishness.

Additional References

- Theory, chapter 11: Elements, Channels, and Centers
- Theory, chapter 13: Adjusting Single-Pointed Focus
- Theory, chapter 18: Meditative Postures
- Theory, chapter 19: Breathing Techniques

Refining Fire Practice

To recover lost focus on the seeing faculty, rest the awareness on the initial anchor to re-establish continuity, then return to the seeing faculty. In time, success with entering the emptiness of seeing itself will improve; be patient.

1. Establish a comfortable meditative posture.
2. Place the thumb of each hand at the base of the ring finger. Collapse the fingers around the thumbs in the form of a fist. The fists lie comfortably

on the upper thighs, palm side facing upward toward the sky.

3. Generate a state of meditative equipoise using resistance breathing (ocean breathing) to ensure the breath is restrained, even, long, slow, and rhythmic. Continue this deep, natural, and gentle belly breath for several moments to relax the mind and body.

4. Choose an object as the initial temporary sight anchor. A picture, the glow of burning incense, a crystal, candle flame, bowl of water; any steady physical object the seeing faculty can be anchored on. Use the anchor to stabilize in the initial portion of the practice, and to re-anchor whenever straying from the object of investigation (the seeing faculty) is noticed.

5. After focusing gently on the initial anchor, draw the awareness back from the anchor and bring it to the nonconceptual sense faculty itself. Let the original anchor blend into the periphery of the background of the perception by perceiving through it and instead resting the awareness on the sense faculty itself.

6. Once a consistent anchor of awareness on the sense faculty has been established, contemplate the notion: "What is seeing?" Allow the awareness to investigate the nature of the sense faculty itself, which is always active, letting go of what is being seen by the sight process; this will help settle the awareness into the sense faculty.

7. Remain in this single-pointed focus with investigative intention on the nonconceptual faculty of seeing as much as possible without straying.

8. Relax and breathe gently and naturally for a few moments to conclude.

Perform this practice for 20–40 minutes each morning during sunrise or in the afternoon during sunset. If these times are not conducive because of lifestyle, the practice can be performed at night, any time before 11:30 pm. Move on when straying only occurs 1–2 times total per session for several sessions in a row.

28

Refining Air

This practice helps one refine the very subtle disturbances related to the element of air and the sense of touch. Remember to rest awareness on the sense faculty with perpetual balance, in the middle, without coercion, stress, or sluggishness.

Additional References

- Theory, chapter 11: Elements, Channels, and Centers
- Theory, chapter 13: Adjusting Single-Pointed Focus
- Theory, chapter 18: Meditative Postures
- Theory, chapter 19: Breathing Techniques

Refining Air Practice

To recover lost focus on the touch faculty, rest the awareness on the initial anchor to re-establish continuity, then return to the touch faculty. In time, success with entering the emptiness of touch itself will improve; be patient.

1. Establish a comfortable meditative posture.
2. The eyes can be positioned naturally and allowed to close gently without any coercion, or they can remain open if this feels more comfortable.

3. Place the thumb of each hand at the base of the ring finger. Collapse the fingers around the thumbs in the form of a fist. The fists lie comfortably on the upper thighs, palm side facing upward toward the sky.

4. Generate a state of meditative equipoise using resistance breathing (ocean breathing) to ensure the breath is restrained, even, long, slow, and rhythmic. Continue this deep, natural, and gentle belly breath for several moments to relax the mind and body.

5. Choose an object as the initial temporary touch (feeling) anchor. This can be a piece of material, a crystal in the hand, the fingers or hands touching, the pants or shirt; any physical object the touch faculty can be anchored on. Use the anchor to stabilize in the initial portion of the practice, and to re-anchor whenever straying from the object of investigation (the feeling or touch faculty) is noticed.

6. After focusing gently on the initial anchor, draw the awareness back from the anchor and bring it to the nonconceptual sense faculty itself. Let the original anchor blend into the periphery of the background of the perception by perceiving through it and instead resting the awareness on the sense faculty itself.

7. Once a consistent anchor of awareness on the sense faculty has been established, contemplate the notion: "What is feeling?" Allow the awareness to investigate the nature of the sense faculty itself, which is always active, letting go of what is being felt by the touch process; this will help settle the awareness into the sense faculty.

8. Remain in this single-pointed focus with investigative intention on the nonconceptual faculty of touch as much as possible without straying.

9. Relax and breathe gently and naturally for a few moments to conclude.

Practice for 20–40 minutes each morning during sunrise or afternoon during sunset. If these times are not conducive because of lifestyle, practice at night, any time before 11:30 pm. Move on when straying only occurs 1–2 times total per session for several sessions in a row.

29

Preliminary View

The preliminary right view differs from the actual right view in that one's preliminary view does not yet contain awareness of the field of nonconceptual emptiness. Later in the method, the full right view is established with the addition of maintaining awareness of emptiness. This practice helps one get used to constantly equalizing phenomena in the awareness in preparation for those later stages.

Approach to Preliminary View Practice

One who is already established in the right view sees all things, even the self, as apparitions in a transient, illusion-like temporal environment, knowing that all will fade out of reality the same way it faded in. This one allows the expression of mindstream and emotional reactions to be seen as the momentary play of the mind. Not running to pleasure or averting from negative states, one simply accepts all expressions at equal value as forms of rhythms from the unconscious mind, making waves on the field of nonconceptual emptiness. This is called focused awareness without attributes.

One who is seeking to establish this pristine perspective aims to first discern a fleeting impression of its emergence, and then to return to it, maintain it, and deepen it. During this initial process, while one still habitually runs toward or away from transient disturbances, it is common to phase in and out of the right view. What one does on recognizing that one has fallen out of the view makes all the difference.

Begin to observe the egoic identity as it continually tries to distinguish the negative from the positive. In each instance where this is noticed, in waking or seated practice, simply remain in (or return to) the view that all experiences are of the exact same nature. This approach helps to further loosen the chains that shackle one to a confused state of perception.

Because rising and falling phenomena have no independent, unique qualities and are equal, it is not helpful to attempt to coerce or fight whatever is arising. Only practice seeing the attractions and aversions for what they are, a natural and neutral function within the body-vehicle that is not part of the essential nature in any way.

To release the generally unconscious and oppressed desires, one must not only become conscious of them, but also come to see them from this purely aware position of neutrality, accepting them as part of the self and disassociating them from the true perceiver awareness. Always return to the right view, neutrally and without coercion. This allows the self to desire whatever it desires without judgment; it separates the self and its desiring, as it is, from the true essential nature. Continued maintenance of the view is simply allowing everything to be just as it is.

This includes allowing one's own thoughts, feelings, sense-desires, speech, and actions to be as they are. It also means allowing the outside world, other people and situations, to come in and out of perception in the same way, just as they are. Everything that is happening is allowed to happen.

Regardless of what people say, or don't say, elect not to coerce or to fight against any reactions. There is no need to struggle against another's words or actions, nor against one's own; everything is left as it is, free. There is also no need to consider right words, morals, dogma, right conditions, etc. Simply give freedom to everything the identity-body wants to do, and give the same freedom to the identity-bodies of others. In allowing everything, self and other, to be free to express, one can easily dismiss the unnecessary judgements of the mind that clutter the view.

Any reactionary emotion that rises up should also be neutrally accepted without any coercion or repression. Whenever reactionary emotions arise, handle these as one would handle a small child—with compassion, patience, and comforting. Allow the identity-body to release and express whatever comes up without any oppression or judgement, maintaining the right view as consistently as possible throughout.

Remember that the self can be what it is, functioning with whatever qualities it has naturally adopted, without one needing to selectively empower some and run from others out of unconscious fear of being associated to the qualities. Let go of the habit of going back after the fact to try and organize, analyze, contemplate, or work with any past or future abstraction about what was or what might be. What is, is.

One's free expression while maintaining the view need not be wild or destructive, however, only genuine. Become very careful with the thoughts, speech (emotions), and actions that are being expressed in each moment. Speech, overthinking, reactionary emotions, and unnecessary movement all have disordering effects on the elemental energies, and one must keep this in mind at this point in the practice. For example, it is best to speak only when it is absolutely necessary, and then only in the most direct way possible, with the least amount of effort.

It is also good to wait 24 hours before addressing any "problem," to be sure that all of the reactionary elements have been discarded. This waiting period allows for careful removal of as much of the unnecessary and unneeded aggressive, defensive, and harmful mental, emotional, and physical action as possible. Reactions fail to actually heal and solve the problem at hand; typically, they only antagonize and create more division.

Whenever the practice is overtaken by mundane matters, driven by unconscious habitual tendencies, it is important to awaken to that loss and return to the right view immediately. Falling out of the view where everything is seen evenly is not an error in itself; falling into reactions that further to ignite these fallen states is the error. Even falling out of the view should be seen as equal to being in it; there should be no distinction or discrimination toward even the slightest wave of thought, speech, or action.

Always return to the view that everything is suchness, a play of the mind, illusory phenomena rising from the nonconceptual field of emptiness between perceiver and perceived. This helps undo the unconscious tendencies that insist on investment and defense of the self.

The states which seem to fluctuate are just reactions, habitual tendencies to see phenomena as something to be fearful of, something to be valued, or something otherwise deemed important. In truth, they are not. Let everything be like the wind on a field of reeds, now blowing this way, now blowing that way, now standing still, and so on—nothing changes for the reeds, they just bend and sway, perfectly.

The Preliminary View practice prepares one for the visionary states through awareness with this right view at four critical energy centers within the body: the heavenly center (over the head, about 24 inches above the crown), the heart center (2 inches inside of the physical heart), the eyes (light), and the ears (sound). It helps open the heart center and the heavenly center, developing the view alongside the right kind of vision and hearing qualities to ensure these faculties can be held correctly, open and vast, paying attention to everything while singling out nothing.

Additional References

- Theory, chapter 12: The Right View
- Theory, chapter 13: Adjusting Single-Pointed Focus
- Theory, chapter 18: Meditative Postures
- Theory, chapter 19: Breathing Techniques

Preliminary View Practice

Do not allow the egoic identity to anticipate or expect anything during this practice; just rest in this condition, knowing that it is working to eradicate subtle habitual tendencies that would otherwise get in the way of full breakthrough.

Take whatever time is needed to build consistent awareness in the energy centers. After some time, awareness of the commingled centers becomes second nature in the moment-by-moment waking state. Establishing a current of multifaceted awareness can take time, so be patient.

If this practice becomes a struggle, try adding just one feature at a time, until able to effortlessly coordinate the heavenly and heart centers together with the view in the background of daily life. If falling out of the view because of unconscious reactions, simply notice the play of illusory phenomena as the cause, and return back to the maintenance of the right view.

1. Establish a comfortable meditative posture.
2. Generate a state of meditative equipoise using resistance breathing (ocean breathing) to ensure the breath is restrained, even, long, slow, and rhythmic. Continue this deep, natural, and gentle belly breath for several moments to relax the mind and body.
3. Install a sense of connection to the heavenly energy center above the head for a few minutes. This connection is subtly maintained throughout the session, and afterward, throughout the day.

4. Raise the thumb up in front of the face and focus the eyes on that area, then let the hand fall back down while retaining focus only on the in-between. Remain in this wide, undistracted view as much as possible throughout the session, and afterward, throughout the day. The view is open and unfocused on anything in particular, seeing everything as a play of illusory rising and falling phenomena, nothing more.

5. While continuing to sense the heavenly center, additionally bring awareness to the heart center, using the field of vision and the sense of hearing as intermediaries. Remain sensing both centers, as if the eyes and ears fasten the heavenly center and the heart center together. Do not overdo this, relax the awareness and let it be subtle, especially in the beginning; no tension or stress.

6. With the centers sensed and commingled, expand the gaze to include a relaxed field of vision that is not focused on anything in particular. Be free of entanglements to mindstream, feelings, sense-desires, speech, and action, allowing the view to go beyond thinking—unfettered, broad, and spacious, without any differentiation of good and bad—this is called awareness with no discrimination, or awareness without attributes.

7. Let awareness of the commingled centers and the view carry over into the periphery of the waking state.

This practice should be used to transition into the waking state each day while continuing with the method, remembering to hold the heavenly-heart connection throughout the day.

30

Earth Arousal

This practice arouses the energy center of earth, which is vital for the successful elimination of element disturbances. The earth (root) center is located at the perineum, between the sexual organ and the anus, below the tip of the spine.

The elemental energies of the body must become stilled to arouse an energy center, so it is important to keep the posture still throughout the practice. Moving the body displaces the elemental energies one is trying to work on.

One's breathing in arousal practices should be most subtle; the breath is eventually so fine and gentle that it is almost imperceptible, and only the directed energy itself is pressing and squeezing into the energy center.

Energy center pressing should not bring on feelings of physical tiredness or wear; these are signs of too much physical exertion. The very gentle and subtle squeezing eventually only occurs by the force of subtle elemental energy; but to start, the pressing can be helped slightly by the muscles in the abdominal walls: in front, pressing backward; at the sides, pressing toward each other; and at the back, pressing forward. This entire process should be calm, natural, relaxed, and gentle at all times. Be sure not to tense the muscles unnecessarily or create any struggle in the body.

Arousal is generally noticed through subtle sensations in the area of the energy center, beyond the physical, and one can look for two key stages of arousal in this practice. The first is ordinary physical sensation, felt once sufficient awareness has been generated in the physical area associated with the energy center. In the second stage, one begins to notice a subtle, unusual sensation that arises after the physical has provided a stable anchor. This second stage of arousal is sufficient for our method.

Additional References

- Theory, chapter 11: Elements, Channels, and Centers
- Theory, chapter 13: Adjusting Single-Pointed Focus
- Theory, chapter 18: Meditative Postures
- Theory, chapter 19: Breathing Techniques

Earth Arousal Practice

Keep the body still, and use only the most subtle breathing and pressing.

1. Establish a comfortable meditative posture.
2. The eyes can be positioned naturally and allowed to close gently without any coercion, or they can remain open if this feels more comfortable.
3. Place the thumb of each hand at the base of the ring finger. Collapse the fingers around the thumbs in the form of a fist. The fists lie comfortably on the upper thighs, palm side facing upward toward the sky.
4. Generate a state of meditative equipoise using resistance breathing (ocean breathing) to ensure the breath is restrained, even, long, slow, and rhythmic. Continue this deep, natural, and gentle belly breath for several moments to relax the mind and body.
5. Focus the awareness at the earth center by imagining a thumb-sized egg there. Keep the awareness here throughout the entire practice.
6. Inhale rhythmically, with long but relaxed and natural breathing, while very gently and subtly tightening the abdominal walls and breathing

energy down into the earth center, condensing the energy there.

7. After the inhalation, retain the breath while continuing the very gentle squeezing; maintain the retention for as long as possible without feeling any laboring for breath, or any tension or stress in the body at all.

8. When ready, release the retained air left in the lungs while continuing to condense the energy to arouse the dormant earth center. In time, there will be a feeling of energy rising up toward the water and fire centers.

9. Repeat from step 6.

10. Relax and breathe gently and naturally for a few moments to conclude.

Perform this practice each day for 20–30 minutes at a time. When subtle energy sensation occurs within the first few minutes during each practice session, feel free to move on.

31

Water Arousal

T his practice arouses the energy center of water. The water (sacral) center is located in front of the spine at the sacrum, near vertebrae S1 and S2, 5 finger-widths above the tip of the spine.

Additional References

- Theory, chapter 11: Elements, Channels, and Centers
- Theory, chapter 13: Adjusting Single-Pointed Focus
- Theory, chapter 18: Meditative Postures
- Theory, chapter 19: Breathing Techniques

Water Arousal Practice

Keep the body still, and use only the most subtle breathing and pressing.

1. Establish a comfortable meditative posture.
2. The eyes can be positioned naturally and allowed to close gently without any coercion, or they can remain open if this feels more comfortable.
3. Place the thumb of each hand at the base of the ring finger. Collapse the fingers around the thumbs in the form of a fist. The fists lie comfortably on the upper thighs, palm side facing upward toward the sky.

4. Generate a state of meditative equipoise using resistance breathing (ocean breathing) to ensure the breath is restrained, even, long, slow, and rhythmic. Continue this deep, natural, and gentle belly breath for several moments to relax the mind and body.

5. Focus the awareness at the water center by imagining a thumb-sized egg there. Keep the awareness here throughout the entire practice.

6. Inhale rhythmically, with long but relaxed and natural breathing, while very gently and subtly tightening the abdominal walls and breathing energy into the water center, condensing the energy there.

7. After the inhalation, retain the breath while continuing the very gentle squeezing; maintain the retention for as long as possible without feeling any laboring for breath, or any tension or stress in the body at all.

8. When ready, release the retained air left in the lungs while continuing to condense the energy into the water center to arouse the dormant energy. In time, there will be a feeling of energy rising outward toward the pubic bone.

9. Repeat from step 6.

10. Relax and breathe gently and naturally for a few moments to conclude.

Perform this practice each day for 20–30 minutes at a time. When subtle energy sensation occurs within the first few minutes during each practice session, feel free to move on.

32

Fire Arousal

This practice arouses the energy center of fire. The fire (solar plexus) center is located in front of the spine, directly behind the navel, near vertebrae L3 and L4.

Additional References

- Theory, chapter 11: Elements, Channels, and Centers
- Theory, chapter 13: Adjusting Single-Pointed Focus
- Theory, chapter 18: Meditative Postures
- Theory, chapter 19: Breathing Techniques

Fire Arousal Practice

Keep the body still, and use only the most subtle breathing and pressing.

1. Establish a comfortable meditative posture.
2. The eyes can be positioned naturally and allowed to close gently without any coercion, or they can remain open if this feels more comfortable.
3. Place the thumb of each hand at the base of the ring finger. Collapse the fingers around the thumbs in the form of a fist. The fists lie comfortably on the upper thighs, palm side facing upward toward the sky.

4. Generate a state of meditative equipoise using resistance breathing (ocean breathing) to ensure the breath is restrained, even, long, slow, and rhythmic. Continue this deep, natural, and gentle belly breath for several moments to relax the mind and body.
5. Focus the awareness at the fire center by imagining a thumb-sized egg there. Keep the awareness here throughout the entire practice.
6. Inhale rhythmically, with long but relaxed and natural breathing, while very gently and subtly tightening the abdominal walls and breathing energy into the fire center, condensing the energy there.
7. After the inhalation, retain the breath while continuing the very gentle squeezing; maintain the retention for as long as possible without feeling any laboring for breath, or any tension or stress in the body at all.
8. When ready, release the retained air left in the lungs while continuing this pressing into the fire center to arouse the dormant energy. In time, there will be a feeling of energy rising forward toward the solar plexus and upward toward the sternum.
9. Repeat from step 6.
10. Relax and breathe gently and naturally for a few moments to conclude.

Perform this practice each day for 20–30 minutes at a time. When subtle energy sensation occurs within the first few minutes during each practice session, feel free to move on.

33

Bliss-Warmth

Bliss-warmth is a fundamental practice that is used throughout the method, from this point forward. Bliss-warmth creates ease and subtle pleasure in the system, helping to relax the body during practice so that it does not disturb the view. It is also a major factor in opening up one's heart space and the barrier restricting it, another crucial stage in advancement.

Bliss-warmth is best activated after one's earth, water, and fire energy centers have been aroused, as both the water and fire elemental energies are required for this practice. Before continuing on to the air and space centers, one must learn to generate bliss-warmth.

Specific breathing in conjunction with the ascending and descending energies of fire and water causes a sort of spark when the energies unite, like two flint stones being struck together. This spark ignites the warmth, which is later directed into the heart for its arousal—a critical secret to the upcoming vision practices. Many teachings on tummo, chandali, kundalini, or inner heat suggest forceful breathing practices, but this is not necessary. In fact, the more subtly the breath is stirred, the more strongly the subtle elemental energies can be lured into union for bliss-warmth.

During the Central Channel practice, one became accustomed to the movement of the various elemental energies, including the water (descending) and fire (ascending) energies. In this practice, one changes the direction of each of these elemental energies, driving them together.

Additional References

- Theory, chapter 11: Elements, Channels, and Centers
- Theory, chapter 13: Adjusting Single-Pointed Focus
- Theory, chapter 18: Meditative Postures
- Theory, chapter 19: Breathing Techniques

Bliss-Warmth Practice

Its essential not to use too much physical exertion in the beginning; this can cause energetic congestion in the subtle body. The body must be totally relaxed, and the energies lured and aroused without any strain or stress. The feeling should be sweet and sensual, similar to sexual arousal.

If additional stabilization is needed in this practice, imagine a small hot coal or flame in the anchor points. If the bliss-warmth starts to decrease at any time during the meditation, return to subtle striking of the water and fire elements until it is re-ignited and re-established.

1. Establish a comfortable meditative posture.
2. The eyes can be positioned naturally and allowed to close gently without any coercion, or they can remain open if this feels more comfortable.
3. Place the thumb of each hand at the base of the ring finger. Collapse the fingers around the thumbs in the form of a fist. The fists lie comfortably on the upper thighs, palm side facing upward toward the sky.
4. Generate a state of meditative equipoise using resistance breathing (ocean breathing) to ensure the breath is restrained, even, long, slow, and rhythmic. Continue this deep, natural, and gentle belly breath for

several moments to relax the mind and body.

5. During inhalation, reverse the ascending energy and lure it downward toward the navel (fire center). This can be felt in the back near the spine, or in some cases more toward the front of the body at the solar plexus; use discernment. If it helps, while inhaling, imagine two small balls of red light that enter the nostrils, wrap around the head, and lower down into the body through the solar and lunar channels, meeting together to unify in the navel center.

6. When the inhalation is complete, comfortably retain the breath for a few moments, holding the ascending fire energy at the navel without physical or mental strain or stress.

7. Gently squeeze the energy in the navel center by drawing the navel and solar plex area back very subtly, to compress the energy. After some time practicing this, no physical muscular involvement will be required.

8. During exhalation, lure the descending water energy upward into the same spot that the fire element was held during retention in step 6.

9. When exhalation is complete, comfortably retain the breath for a few moments, compressing the water energy at the same location that the fire energy was held, without physical or mental strain or stress.

10. Repeat this process of striking the fire and water elements with breath retention until the spark of bliss-warmth can be felt in the navel (solar plexus) with stability. Later, when stability is reached, gradually relax the need for the striking; the bliss-warmth will begin to maintain itself through single-pointed focus on the anchor, without the assistance of the breath.

11. Relax and breathe gently and naturally for a few moments to conclude.

Spend 20–30 minutes each day practicing the ignition of bliss-warmth until it can be easily ignited and the sensation is retained throughout the practice without additional striking. At that point it is time to move on to the next practice.

34

Air Arousal

This practice arouses the air center, which is related to the heart space. The air (heart) center is located between the breasts, and between the shoulder blades in the back near the T7, T8, and T9 vertebrae in front of the spine. The awareness is held at this point during the practice, in the heart itself, to ensure the energy is flowing to the right center. It can be useful to visualize a 2-inch green egg within the heart, to stabilize awareness.

This practice is critical for the visions needed to refine the very subtle elemental energies so the heart can ultimately reunite with the mind's eye. The eyes and the heart are intimately connected; where the eye flows, the heart goes. The heart-mind connection is disturbed by the elemental energies. This leads to unnecessary stirring of mindstream, which in turn causes reactionary emotions, and this influences speech and actions which ultimately shape and form the outside macrocosmic environment. The unification of the subtle heart center and mind's eye restores balance and creates a state of pristine clarity.

Arousal of the air center will cause the stirring of emotional energy. Sometimes this stirring occurs moments after practice or not at all, and other times hours later, or even the next day. The arousal of emotional energies may come as positive, warm, and compassionate feelings, or it can come in the form of annoyance, anger, depression, or other kinds of negatively felt emotions. Do not restrict the energy once it arises; the objective is to relax and release these energies, not to suppress them back into restriction. It is important to notice these expressions and breathe through them with deep, slow, and rhythmic breaths, until the energy disperses naturally. If the energies rise up again soon after, simply repeat the breathing process, helping them to release in a calm, relaxed, and conscious way.

Additional References

- Theory, chapter 11: Elements, Channels, and Centers
- Theory, chapter 13: Adjusting Single-Pointed Focus
- Theory, chapter 18: Meditative Postures
- Theory, chapter 19: Breathing Techniques
- Practice, chapter 33: Bliss-Warmth

Air Arousal Practice

Keep the body still, and use only the most subtle breathing and pressing.

1. Establish a comfortable meditative posture.
2. The eyes can be positioned naturally and allowed to close gently without any coercion, or they can remain open if this feels more comfortable.
3. Place the thumb of each hand at the base of the ring finger. Collapse the fingers around the thumbs in the form of a fist. The fists lie comfortably on the upper thighs, palm side facing upward toward the sky.
4. Generate a state of meditative equipoise using resistance breathing (ocean breathing) to ensure the breath is restrained, even, long, slow, and rhythmic. Continue this deep, natural, and gentle belly breath for several moments to relax the mind and body.
5. When ready, generate some bliss-warmth at the fire center, underneath the opening bell of the central channel.

6. Take some time to slowly and gently lure the bliss-warmth from the navel (fire center) up into the central channel, so that it begins to climb up toward the air center in the heart.

7. Let the bliss-warmth abide for a few moments at the restriction near the heart, to help relax it.

8. Slowly and gently lure the bliss-warmth past the barrier and into the air center itself, into the heart; visualize a 2-inch green egg within the heart itself, if that is helpful.

9. Stay aware of the bliss-warmth at the heart throughout the remainder of the practice: sense/feel the fire center generating the bliss-warmth, its flow up to the heart, and the heart center receiving it.

10. Relax and breathe gently and naturally for a few moments to conclude.

Continue this exercise each day for at least 20–30 minutes. When a joyful, calm, and radiant sensation is felt within the air center (heart), expanding outward with a deeply penetrative expression of energy, and this sensation occurs in the same quality over several meditations in a row, move on to the next practice.

35

Space Arousal

This practice arouses the space element, which is the source of hearing and is intimately connected to the throat. The space (throat) center is located between the pit of the throat in the front, and the c4 and c5 vertebrae in the neck. The awareness is held at this point during the practice to ensure the energy is flowing to the right center.

Resting awareness continually at this center while driving the warm energy from the navel up to this point causes a quick arousal, which plays a critical role in the continuation of the path.

Arousing this subtle space element is an important factor for activating the channel that will later be used to unite the heart center and the mind's eye.

Additional References

- Theory, chapter 11: Elements, Channels, and Centers
- Theory, chapter 13: Adjusting Single-Pointed Focus
- Theory, chapter 18: Meditative Postures
- Theory, chapter 19: Breathing Techniques
- Practice, chapter 33: Bliss-Warmth

Space Arousal Practice

Keep the body still, and use only the most subtle breathing and pressing.

1. Establish a comfortable meditative posture.
2. The eyes can be positioned naturally and allowed to close gently without any coercion, or they can remain open if this feels more comfortable.
3. Generate a deep state of meditative equipoise using the long, rhythmic resistance breathing deep into the belly. The awareness should follow the breath as it enters the body, fills the belly and exits the body until the body and mind calm down.
4. Place the thumb of each hand at the base of the ring finger. Collapse the fingers around the thumbs in the form of a fist. The fists lie comfortably on the upper thighs, palm side facing upward toward the sky.
5. When ready, generate some bliss-warmth at the fire center, underneath the opening bell of the central channel.
6. Take some time to slowly and gently lure the bliss-warmth from the navel (fire center) up into the central channel, so that it begins to climb up toward the space center at the throat.
7. Let the bliss-warmth abide for a few moments at the restriction near the throat, to help relax it.
8. Slowly and gently lure the bliss-warmth past the barrier and into the space center itself, at the throat; visualize a small green egg within the throat, if that is helpful.
9. Stay aware of the bliss-warmth at the throat throughout the remainder of the practice: sense/feel the space center generating the bliss-warmth, its flow up to the throat, and the space center receiving it.
10. Relax and breathe gently and naturally for a few moments to conclude.

Continue this exercise each day for at least 20–30 minutes. When a stimulating, tingling vibration is felt at the space center, expanding outward with powerful stimulating energy in the same quality over several meditations in a row, move on to Clear Light Mystic Vision.

36

Clear Light Mystic Vision

Vision practices must be understood well and should only be performed by the suitably prepared practitioner, one that has spent adequate time building the proper foundation. If one's foundation is not sufficient, these practices will cause frustration and disappointment, or worse. If, however, one has fortified the foundation and gained proficiency prior to attempting these practices, one will discover the breakthrough point in the gateway that leads to profound luminous clarity.

This practice requires a natural light source; it can be performed in a room that has windows, but even better if one can be outside, facing a wide open sky. The most important aspect is to choose an area that is as free from disturbance as possible, noiseless and solitary, with only the sound of nature in the background. The practice area should be protected from sudden interruptions which will ruin this effort.

This should be done one hour before or after sunrise or sunset. Face the sun at an angle, putting it off to the right or left of the vision by at least 45 degrees; do not stare at the sun, since that can be damaging to the eyes. If being in direct sunlight is too intense for any reason, it is possible to turn further away from the sun (up to 90 degrees), or simply perform the practice indoors.

Make sure there is enough space to get into all of the postures easily and without difficulty. Try to cycle through all five postures in each session, but if one or two specific postures feel more seamless and easy to orient to in the beginning, start with sessions containing only those postures. The other, more complex postures can be added over time, working up to all five in each session.

For the practice to be successful, it is vital that the right view is held. Each moment that the correct view is maintained radically reformats the attributes of the elemental energies that disturb the system. If the right view is not maintained, the practice becomes powerless and ineffective.

The correct gaze can be reestablished by looking up at the sky until unfocused small anomalies are revealed that look like lines of light darting around in the intermediate vision (not external, not internal).

During this practice, one makes the intention to notice the experience of nonconceptual emptiness; this can arise at any time, especially in the more advanced stages of the practice. Continual noticing helps keep the awareness away from playing with the forms of phenomena that will fill the secret visions, and it begins to cause the separation of awareness from the identity-body so that emptiness can become known.

In this total relaxed state of maintaining the view during each posture, one contemplates the sensation of nonconceptual, nondual emptiness, what the state of self-emptiness feels like beyond the senses, beyond the mind. This is repeated throughout the meditation whenever a deep, satiated state of selflessness has been achieved. The impression created during this meditative practice is an important part of transferring the special perception self-emptiness into the waking state later on in the method.

Remember to keep the body and eyes still, and use only the most subtle breathing necessary.

Additional References

- Theory, chapter 11: Elements, Channels, and Centers
- Theory, chapter 12: The Right View
- Theory, chapter 13: Adjusting Single-Pointed Focus
- Theory, chapter 15: Mystical Visions
- Theory, chapter 18: Meditative Postures
- Theory, chapter 19: Breathing Techniques
- Practice, chapter 33: Bliss-Warmth

Clear Light Mystic Vision Practice

Each of the vision postures should be held for 5 minutes to start, and the duration can be increased at each session as this process becomes more fluid and comfortable.

1. Establish a comfortable meditative posture.
2. For the first part of this practice, the eyes can be positioned naturally and allowed to close gently without any coercion, or they can remain open if this feels more comfortable.
3. For the first part of this practice, place the thumb of each hand at the base of the ring finger. Collapse the fingers around the thumbs in the form of a fist. The fists lie comfortably on the upper thighs, palm side facing upward toward the sky.
4. Generate a state of meditative equipoise using resistance breathing (ocean breathing) to ensure the breath is restrained, even, long, slow, and rhythmic. Continue this deep, natural, and gentle belly breath for several moments to relax the mind and body.
5. Arouse bliss-warmth at the navel center.
6. Lure the bliss-warmth into the heart center to arouse it. Bliss-warmth should be maintained in the heart center throughout the rest of the meditative session (all postures).

7. Optionally, lure the bliss-warmth further to the throat center to arouse it as well.

8. Become aware of and establish the hearing faculty.

9. Divided in equal time, begin cycling through the vision postures, including the breathing instructions that follow. While holding each posture, maintain bliss-warmth in the fire, air, and space centers while also ensuring the gaze is correct by seeing everything but never focusing on any phenomenon in particular. The gaze is key! Keep both the body and the eyes motionless, with the eyes as still and unblinking as possible. Eye stillness will improve as the practice continues and the elemental energies refine. Holding the right view here is paramount.

10. In the beginning of each posture, with every few inhalations or so, effortlessly retain the breath (stop the inhalation short) at 50% air capacity for 20–60 seconds without strain or stress of any kind. This retention should include the fire element being pressed down from the navel toward the water energy that rises up from near the tip of the spine.

11. At the end of these beginning inhalations, retain the breath while gently pulling the navel back toward the spine.

12. Keep retaining these breaths during the beginning phase of each gazing posture; take a few soft and gentle natural breaths before repeating the retention process from step 10.

13. After half the meditative time has passed, per posture, allow the breath to be natural again, completely relaxed and without retention.

14. Whenever a deep, satiated state of selflessness arrives in each posture, contemplate the sensation of nonconceptual, nondual emptiness, what the state of self-emptiness feels like beyond the senses, beyond the mind.

15. Repeat through all vision postures from step 5.

16. Relax and breathe gently and naturally for a few moments to conclude.

Do a vision session once per day, either in the morning near or at sunrise or later in the afternoon near or at sunset, for 25 minutes or more (building up as time goes on). Once indicators begin to arise for the second stage of visionary experiences, where subtle visions like fog, heat-like waves, static, motionless light, wavy flames, and other visual anomalies become more regular, clear, and intense, it is time to move on and begin the Dark Light Mystic Vision practice (chapter 38).

Preliminary Dream Projection (chapter 37) can be started concurrent with the vision practices.

37

Preliminary Dream Projection

This process begins to awaken dream lucidity, and it is used in conjunction with the vision practices which are already helping to eradicate the very subtle elemental energy disturbances.

Firm establishment of preliminary waking view is required, where all perceived phenomena is seen as a dream-like play of the mind. All objects in the vision, people in the perception, and the environment itself are as illusory dream-like projections that rise and fall out of the field. Routinely remember during waking life that this is a dream, and feel it as such. Everything is impermanent, transient, and therefore illusory.

Dream Projection practice continues through the Clear Light and Dark Light Mystic Vision practices. Success is not important here, only that the practice is used as described. As vision practices continue, dream lucidity should occur more naturally and consistently. This dream practice also becomes a meter for progress.

Additional References

- Theory, chapter 12: The Right View
- Theory, chapter 18: Meditative Postures

- Theory, chapter 19: Breathing Techniques
- Practice, chapter 25: Gift-Blessings Offering
- Practice, chapter 33: Bliss-Warmth

Preliminary Dream Projection Practice

1. Before bed, perform devotional offerings/prayers to the governing force known as *Chamuel* or *Chamuana*, requesting aid to maintain wakeful awareness during dreams and throughout the night. The days of the 5th and 11th lunar houses, in each cycle, can be especially helpful for this practice.

2. Wake at 4:30 am.

3. Establish the comfortable sleep posture for this practice.

4. Generate a state of meditative equipoise using resistance breathing (ocean breathing) to ensure the breath is restrained, even, long, slow, and rhythmic. Continue this deep, natural, and gentle belly breath for several moments to relax the mind and body.

5. Generate very subtle bliss-warmth in the lower body.

6. Use visualization to subtly stimulate some arousal in the body. Listen to the companion lectures for more details on this step.

7. Bring the focus to the throat center and the hearing faculty itself.

8. Imagine a small black seed sitting in the throat center.

9. Fall asleep gently, while remaining focused on the black seed in the throat center. Do not be afraid; the arousal energy will help overcome fear. Make sure the body is comfortable and totally relaxed, calm, and not anticipating anything. Expectation causes egoic stirring, making it troublesome to fall back to sleep. Allow the arousal energy to generate a calm, joyful expression in the body.

10. Generate visions as instructed in the mystic vision practice (chapter 36), but do not focus on them; keep the gaze unfocused on anything in particular. As the visions emerge, relax, allowing them to come and go while drifting back into sleep.

11. On awakening, do not jump out of bed; simply remain still and focus

on the heart center, gently meditating there for a few moments.

12. Arise and write or record any significant experiences, being as detailed as possible.

Repeat this practice as much as possible without disrupting work, home, or school involvement relative to sleep needs. Every other day, or even 2 times per week is sufficient. Continue this practice until it is time to move into the Dream and Deep Sleep View.

38

Dark Light Mystic Vision

This practice requires a dark space to further develop and deepen the visionary stages. This can be done in a room with very low light, or it can be done outside at night. The most important aspect is to choose an area that is as free from disturbance as possible, noiseless and solitary, with only the sound of nature in the background. The practice area should be protected from sudden interruptions which will ruin this effort.

If the practice is done outside, face the moon at an angle, putting it off to the right or left of the vision by at least 45 degrees. If done indoors, place a soft warm light, such as a candle or ghee/oil lamp, on the floor 5–8 feet ahead. This establishes a small amount of available light which can be used for gazing downward, directly over, straight ahead, or up higher, depending on the eye position related to each posture.

Make sure there is enough space to get into all of the postures easily and without difficulty. Try to cycle through all five postures in each session, but if one or two specific postures feel more seamless and easy to orient to in the beginning, start with sessions containing only those postures. The other, more complex postures can be added over time, working up to all five in each session.

For the practice to be successful, it is vital that the right view is held. Each moment that the correct view is maintained radically reformats the attributes of the elemental energies that disturb the system. If the right view is not maintained, the practice becomes powerless and ineffective.

During this practice, one makes the intention to notice the experience of nonconceptual emptiness; this can arise at any time, especially in the more advanced stages of the practice. Continual noticing helps keep the awareness away from playing with the forms of phenomena that will fill the secret visions, and it begins to cause the separation of awareness from the identity-body so that emptiness can become known.

In this total relaxed state of maintaining the view during each posture, one contemplates the sensation of nonconceptual, nondual emptiness, what the state of self-emptiness feels like beyond the senses, beyond the mind. This is repeated throughout the meditation whenever a deep, satiated state of selflessness has been achieved. The impression created during this meditative practice is an important part of transferring the special perception self-emptiness into the waking state later on in the method.

Remember to keep the body and eyes still, and use only the most subtle breathing necessary.

Additional References

- Theory, chapter 11: Elements, Channels, and Centers
- Theory, chapter 12: The Right View
- Theory, chapter 13: Adjusting Single-Pointed Focus
- Theory, chapter 15: Mystical Visions
- Theory, chapter 18: Meditative Postures
- Theory, chapter 19: Breathing Techniques
- Practice, chapter 33: Bliss-Warmth

Dark Light Mystic Vision Practice

Each of the vision postures should be held for 5 minutes to start, and the duration can be increased at each session as this process becomes more fluid and comfortable.

1. Establish a comfortable meditative posture.
2. For the first part of this practice, the eyes can be positioned naturally and allowed to close gently without any coercion, or they can remain open if this feels more comfortable.
3. For the first part of this practice, place the thumb of each hand at the base of the ring finger. Collapse the fingers around the thumbs in the form of a fist. The fists lie comfortably on the upper thighs, palm side facing upward toward the sky.
4. Generate a state of meditative equipoise using resistance breathing (ocean breathing) to ensure the breath is restrained, even, long, slow, and rhythmic. Continue this deep, natural, and gentle belly breath for several moments to relax the mind and body.
5. Arouse bliss-warmth at the navel center.
6. Lure the bliss-warmth into the heart center to arouse it. Bliss-warmth should be maintained in the heart center throughout the rest of the meditative session (all postures).
7. Optionally, lure the bliss-warmth further to the throat center to arouse it as well.
8. Become aware of and establish the hearing faculty.
9. Divided in equal time, begin cycling through the vision postures, including the breathing instructions that follow. While holding each posture, maintain bliss-warmth in the fire, air, and space centers while also ensuring the gaze is correct by seeing everything but never focusing on any phenomenon in particular. The gaze is key! Keep both the body and the eyes motionless, with the eyes as still and unblinking as possible. Eye stillness will improve as the practice continues and the elemental energies refine. Holding the right view here is paramount.

10. In the beginning of each posture, with every few inhalations or so, effortlessly retain the breath (stop the inhalation short) at 50% air capacity for 20–60 seconds without strain or stress of any kind. This retention should include the fire element being pressed down from the navel toward the water energy that rises up from near the tip of the spine.

11. At the end of these beginning inhalations, retain the breath while gently pulling the navel back toward the spine.

12. Keep retaining these breaths during the beginning phase of each gazing posture; take a few soft and gentle natural breaths before repeating the retention process from step 10.

13. After half the meditative time has passed, per posture, allow the breath to be natural again, completely relaxed and without retention.

14. Whenever a deep, satiated state of selflessness arrives in each posture, contemplate the sensation of nonconceptual, nondual emptiness, what the state of self-emptiness feels like beyond the senses, beyond the mind.

15. Repeat through all vision postures from step 5.

16. Relax and breathe gently and naturally for a few moments to conclude.

Do a vision session once per night, any time after sunset and up until 11:30 pm, for 25 minutes or more (building up as time goes on). Once indicators arise for the fourth stage of visionary experiences, where the connecting-seeds at each joint in the lattice begin to open into the heavenly fields, it is time to move on to Dream and Deep Sleep View.

Preliminary Dream Projection (chapter 37) can be maintained concurrent with this vision practice.

39

Dream and Deep Sleep View

With the handle of authentic emptiness gripped, and lucid dreaming states effortlessly and automatically emerging, it is time to discuss the proper way to approach dream lucidity and deep sleep in a way that will remove the most subtle elemental energy disturbances.

In this practice, one establishes a strong connection between the awareness and emptiness so that awareness perceives emptiness as the dominant state of being. This is crucial so that the final union of awareness and emptiness can be attained, causing the end of the path: sealed stream-realization.

One learns how to work within the dreaming and deep sleep states for the sake of deepening both the perception of the field of emptiness as well as the strength of awakened awareness, so that the final union is much faster, more effective, and seamlessly accessible without hindrances.

The approach to dream and deep sleep awareness should be understood thoroughly through interaction with a teacher, if at all possible. There are many nuances that cannot be explained here, and the finer points of the instructions are better served through direct explanation from someone who has already accomplished the task.

Being awakened in the dream and deep sleep states with the right view means that one is totally free from the bondage of death and rebirth forever. Where conceptual thought gently drifts away, in its place come the heavenly fields of naturally occurring simplistic brilliance.

Emptiness is like the clear blue sky, and awakened awareness is like the sun radiating in the infinitely pure universe of illumination. When the two of these inevitably unite, they remain in seamless perpetual unique unity. In this state, the driving factors of ego-attachment and the anticipation of transient sense-desire fulfillment have fallen away forever.

To help remove the final strata of most subtle disturbances, it is vital that one maintains the right view in dreaming, and later in deep sleep, much like one does in the waking and gazing (vision) states. Disturbances are removed automatically with continuous resting in the revelation of authentic nonconceptual emptiness.

Adherence to emptiness must be accompanied by the right state of awareness. The seeing principle must be free, clear, and vast, recognizing all rising and falling phenomena equally, without distinction or discrimination. When one remains in the waking view, where awakened awareness is experiencing emptiness throughout the day and night, this is called perfect awareness without attributes, or primordial awareness without distinction.

This view does not mean thoughts, feelings or sense-desires do not arise within the dream, it simply means that one's association to these rising and falling phenomena is now different. This difference in association is what ultimately helps snap the shackles, the subtle entanglements, that reinforce the ego-awareness attachment. Whenever this view is lost to phenomena-chasing in waking, dreams, or deep sleep, it is critical to recognize this and return immediately, regardless of how fascinating or important the environmental conditions seem to be.

The key is in not deviating from this view, which should be effortless and completely relaxed at all times. If one is still allowing the mind to leap from point to point, driving attention compulsively from one phenomenon to another, this reinforces entanglements and further disturbs the energies by causing restrictions within the channels. Whatever arises in the eyes, the ears, the mind, or the body should all appear as having no center, no fixed point; all is a continuous play of the rising and falling of the same dream-like substance coming from the nonconceptual emptiness, the field of perception. Everything should be held as one waving illusion on the ocean of perception. Maintaining and deepening this continuum of open and clear perception further reduces attachments and loosens restrictions caused by elemental energies which had reified awareness into the entanglement of identity-body.

Holding the same clear, open, and unfettered view of emptiness in one's waking, meditative, and dreaming states blends the meditative state into waking life more thoroughly. Even anticipation, expectation, very subtle negative or positive judgements, fulfillment of sense-desires, and hints of reactionary emotions should be perceived clearly, seen through as another equal experience of rising and falling phenomena, not allowed to disturb the view. Each moment that one continues to reinforce emptiness into the perception of the internal and external worlds helps to equalize and unify them evenly; this equalization is allowing them to bleed into each other more and more over time, causing awareness to awaken more deeply.

The recognition of the natural state of the awareness coupled with this equalizing of external and internal experiences further removes stains caused by the elemental energies, and meditative attainments begin to transfer into the waking daily life. This transference is essential for success with the practices of dream and deep sleep.

Having witnessed the heavenly fields and the variety of vivid and profound phenomena there, one is prepared to move into the very intense conditions of dreams and deep sleep for the final breakthrough. Whatever experiences arise in the dream or deep sleep states, one should always maintain attention toward the view of emptiness as the interdependent condition of all phenomena. Over time, the comprehensive right view will become much more seamless, natural and organic. At that point, signs arise that it is time to move on to the final union, and the end of the path.

All mental projections which had created the various "environments" one perceived during dreaming drop away. All that remains is an unexplainable clear state, a deeply powerful continuous unchanging landscape of clarity, which is the attainment of deep sleep awareness.

Once dreaming projections are cleared from the field of perception, and awareness maintains its clear view, union is all that remains; sealed stream-realization is very close at hand.

Lectures and one-on-one counsel are essential to understand the subtle points of this view; please be sure to comprehend the right conditions necessary for this process before attempting it.

40

Sealing Realization

R eaching this phase of the path is a rare feat for human beings—congratulations. Drukama teachers are more than happy to personally assist you
in navigating the remainder of the process, if you need help with union.
Don't feel alone in this final, most important step.

* * *

Eliminating many of the subtle, very subtle, and most subtle disturbing
elemental energies (that had driven unconscious attachments to the identity-
body), one reaches a point of stable, clear, and natural mind, heart, and
body.

The perception of the field of nonconceptual authentic emptiness will have
emerged in perception, and it cannot be unseen or lost; it was always there,
and it will always be there.

All that remains for one to seal the realized state of perception is to perform
the penetrative view of insight (awakened awareness held with intention)
toward the field until awareness unifies with it completely. With this, the
path is complete. Do not coerce this critical last step prior to fulfilling the
previous steps; it is impossible and will only cause great misfortune.

Before moving into the correct process of the union of awakened awareness and the field of nonconceptual emptiness, it is important to address one more vital point.

It is very common for the practitioner to feel like there is nothing left to do once the desires have been transmigrated and the identity-body is no longer disturbing the awakened awareness. One can easily reside in a peaceful state of joyful perception without much aspiration to do anything else. However, overestimating one's position at this stage would be a critical error.

Even for one who has reached a pristine condition of radiant clarity and has experienced and interacted within the most subtle dimensions, if the final union of insight and emptiness are not accomplished, none of it will last.

The process is simple enough, but the path will be prolonged unnecessarily if one has the wrong type of intention, misunderstands the application of insight, does not hold the right aspiration consistently, or fails to realize the overall function. After all of the work that was done to generate a supreme stage of preparedness, full understanding of the right approach is not only important, it is critical for sealing stream-realization permanently.

The most effective and fail-proof way to gain understanding about generating the correct state of insight is to hear from a teacher who has already performed it. There is a certain essence and delivery that is important for someone approaching this stage, and that comes through much more efficiently while actively listening to someone who has accomplished it, instead of just reading about, or, heaven forbid, guessing about this very subtle state of investigation.

With the platform of the field of non-conceptual emptiness wide open, accessible for the field of awareness to unify with, one adjusts awareness to contain a specific intention: a penetrative motivation that the awareness seeks to look at and understand by embedding with it more and more.

This penetrative seal being created by the awareness toward the field of nonconceptual emptiness must be held consistently, with the aspiration that nothing else takes precedent over this goal of attainment.

This intention to know is driven by the feeling of separation between the two, like a child who was lost, finally seeing its mother across the field and wanting to be with her. This aspiration comes from knowing that the only thing left to do is to make the two into one in holy matrimony, the alchemical wedding, the sacred union of male and female (deities) that become the one uniquely unified whole.

It is important to hold this aspiration in the most subtle and most gentle way, but also in the most fervently persistent way. Time is all that is needed now; there is no more meditation, no more path, no more adjustment, no more effort beyond this. The maintenance of this view happens continually, at the forefront of perception, while the rest of waking and resting reality happens in the periphery.

Now the field of nonconceptual emptiness becomes like a handle, and awareness like the hand. They both begin to turn in union, and eventually they become one. A bird soaring through the sky is like the awakened awareness, and the sky is like the primordial field of perceiving pure emptiness. They work together effortlessly, so that neither is complete without the other, and they truly are one. Without the sky, the bird cannot fly; without the bird, the sky serves no function on its own.

To sustain this persistent focus, it is good to be away from disturbances, mundane matters, and trivial dramas that draw one away from the union. If previous practices were accomplished proficiently and completely, then the strength and prominence of the field of emptiness and one's powerfully awakened awareness should be no match for worldly theater. In this supreme state of strength, one should not worry much about the transient overcoming the infinite nature, but carefulness is certainly warranted.

The more consistency one can apply, and the stronger the intention used for the union, the less time one spends in contemplation of it. It is only a matter of time before one is liberated from the world of delusion, confusion, and suffering.

41

Conclusion

Achieving the preeminent treasure sought by every fervent and devoted mystic, you will have discovered and passed through the mysterious gateway of emptiness whose barrier lies hidden deep within the primordial unconscious mind.

Entering into the sacred treasury, reuniting awakened awareness with primordial emptiness in holy matrimony, you will have overcome the single greatest challenge presented to each physically incarnated human being.

Revealing what had previously seemed unattainable and inconceivable, you will have earned access to the highest knowledge which transcends the ordinary intellectual mind, effectively moderating the once-concealed supreme functions of the most subtle field of nonconceptual emptiness.

You will have returned home to the garden of Eden; congratulations. Few human beings throughout the ages have been able to claim this victory and gain access to the divine treasury.

It will be essential that you make use of these powerful new mystical gifts. Ensure that you do not go to your bodily grave without sharing these esoteric secrets. Share them with everyone possessing the spiritual *ears to hear* and the aspiration to implement the teachings for virtuous and effective use. It is incumbent on each stream winner to take up the role of guardian of the secret treasury of instructions that have been gifted to you; these gifts are a blessing and anointing from the highest source of All.

As you are already becoming aware of each day, the attainment of realization means you will have been thrust into a larger role within humanity. As a stream-winner, you are required to be a pillar of strength, Light, and connection to the larger unconscious masses.

It is vital that you hold yourself as an intermediary between this world and the others, always attempting to bring joy, knowledge, and mystical medicine to those who need it most. Embracing this role also helps the group establish our right intention for the benefit of those who feel they cannot help themselves; you empower them through appropriate introduction to the mystical ideas that can help them take important evolutionary steps forward. This responsibility comes to you as part of the attainment of realization, and each of us should hold that obligation close to our hearts at all times.

Sealing the realized state, you have joined an elect group of people on Earth (and beyond). You represent an important component of humanity's evolution, and whether you choose to teach openly or work in private, your presence is most needed in our world—bless you. If you wish to teach publicly, please consider lecturing with us at the Drukama Treasury. The demand for authentic instruction is greater than what any individual can accommodate, and we are stronger together; any help is greatly appreciated.

Index

A

Adam 37, *see also* awareness; also mind
adjustment, meditative 69, 74–77, 100,
    101, 111, 112, 114, 119, 181, 182
aggregates 19, 53, 56, 57, 60, 64
air energy center (heart), *see* heart;
    under elemental energy, types
akash, *see* elemental energy: types (space)
All 20, 37, 44, 47, 65, 90, 132, 185,
    see also energy; also Light
altar, *see* gift-blessings; practice area
alternative posture, *see* posture(s): seated
anchor 20, 75–79, 101, 102
ardha padmasana, *see* posture(s): seated
asana, *see* movement practices; posture(s)
astral projection, *see* projection
attachment, *see* entanglement
authentic emptiness, *see* emptiness
authentic mysticism, *see* under path
awakening 3, 8, 13, 17, 18, 34, 37, 41, 42,
    48, 54, 57, 65, 67, *see* also under
    awareness
awareness 7, 8, 11, 12, 16, 17, 19, 22–40,
    43–48, 51, 53–55, 59, 60, 62–64,
    66–81, 83, 85, 87, 91, 99–102, 104,
    176–82, 184, 185, *see also*
    single-pointed focus
    awakened vii, 4, 7, 9, 23–31, 34–38,
        41, 43, 46–48, 54, 55, 61, 63, 65, 67,
        72, 73, 79, 80, 83, 84, 121, 136,
        176–78, 180–82, 184 (*see*
        also insight)
    extraordinary 12, 19, 24, 27, 29, 71
        (*see also* realization)
    ordinary 11, 13, 14, 19, 23, 24, 27, 28,
        37, 184

B

baptism 25, 36, 37
beings 3, 16, 17, 20, 32, 40, 46, 47, 66,
    87, 132–35
bell breathing, *see* under breath
bliss-clarity 38, 61, 63, 68, 81, 112,
    see also union
bliss-warmth 59, 85, 156–58, *see also*
    energy: arousal
body 7, 11, 17, 18, 20, 21, 25, 28, 33, 43,
    44, 47, 50–56, 58, 60, 62, 63, 66, 69,
    70, 76, 77, 79, 83, 85, 86, 92, 96–112,
    135, 144, 180, *see also* identity-body

breath 5, 62, 64, 77, 85, 96–100, 111–15
    bell breath 130–31
    resistance breath (ocean breath) 77
    retention 84, 111

C

cause (root) 7, 8, 12, 14, 18, 21–23, 31,
    39, 42, 45, 58, 64, 82, 86, *see*
    also source
caution, *see* under path
central channel, *see* energy: channel(s)
chakra, *see* energy: center(s)
Chamuana 170
Chamuel 170
Chavah 37
cognition, *see* aggregates
concentration, *see* single-pointed focus
consecration, *see* practice area
correction 7, 8, 12, 20, 24, 73–77, 83, 99,
    101, *see also* adjustment, meditative
creation, structure of 18, 20, 42, 76, 86,
    91, 92, 115
creative principle viii, 3, 20, 21, 45, 53,
    76, 114, 179
cycle(s), *see* under time(s)

D

death 3, 47, 62, 73, 86, 87, *see also*
    rebirth, cycle of
deities, *see* also All; also gift-blessings
    Chamuana 170
    Chamuel 170
    Shakti 37 (*see also* emptiness;
        also heart)
    Shiva 37, 44 (*see also* awareness;
        also mind)
desire 7, 8, 19, 20, 22, 25, 31, 32, 35, 39,
    41, 42, 47, 49–54, 61–66, 69, 70, 75,
    80, 88, 97, 101, 112, 113, 126, 128,
    129, 144, 177, 178, 181
devotion, *see* gift-blessings
dharana, *see* investigation;
    single-pointed focus
dhyana, *see* union
diet, *see* well-being
dimensions, *see* realms
direct experience 7, 8, 17, 18–22, 28, 37,
    38, 46, 47, 51, 59, 63, 78, 80, 132, 176
divinity, *see* All
dream projection, *see* projection

dreaming, *see* under sleep: states
Drukama, *see* path
duality, *see* under perception

E

earth energy center (root), *see* under
    elemental energy, types
easy meditative posture, *see* posture(s):
    meditative, seated
Eden, garden of 28, 38, 46, 184, *see*
    also emptiness
ego, *see* identity-body
ego-boundary, *see* aggregates
elemental energy 25, 31, 58–67, 72, 77,
    79, 80–83, 85, 91, 93–97, 100–102,
    104, 112–15, 119, 126–27, 132–35,
    149–67, 172–76, *see* also aggregates;
    also energy
sub-elements 62–65, 113
    types (*see* also posture(s): mystic
    vision)
        air 58, 60–64, 66, 84, 85, 93, 94,
            101, 105, 109, 113, 114, 127,
            141–42, 159–61
        earth 58, 60–64, 66, 86, 93, 101,
            104, 106, 113, 114, 127, 149–51
        fire 58, 60–64, 66, 86, 93–94, 101,
            105, 108, 113, 114, 127, 131,
            139–40, 154–58
        space 27, 32, 35, 36, 58, 60, 62–66,
            72, 84, 85, 101, 105, 110, 113–15,
            127, 132, 136–38, 162–63
        water 58–64, 66, 86, 93–95, 101,
            104, 107, 113, 114, 127, 152–53,
            156–58
emotion 6, 12–14, 22, 25, 35, 40, 51, 58,
    60, 61, 63, 66, 71, 75, 80, 88, 100, 101,
    111–15, 123, 126, 128–29, 143, 145,
    146, 159–60, 178
empowerment, *see* energy
emptiness vii, 7, 8, 11, 19, 21, 25–38, 40,
    42–49, 53, 55, 60, 65, 68–75, 78–81,
    84–87, 101, 143, 146, 165, 169, 173,
    176–82, 184
energy, *see* also elemental energy;
    also Light
    activation (*see* energy: arousal)
    arousal 31, 84, 102, 149–63 (*see*
        also bliss-warmth)

center(s) 31, 58–61, 81–85, 136–42,
    146–63
channel(s) 25, 58–61, 80, 81, 83, 85,
    100, 102, 111, 112, 123–25, 130–31,
    178
    main (central, right, left) 61, 102,
        111, 112, 123–25, 130–31
cycle(s) (*see* under time(s))
lunar (energy) 61, 92–95, 112, 113, 115
    (*see* also energy: channel(s); also
    lunar (moon); also under lunar; also
    under time(s))
movement 42, 58, 59, 119–22
purification 81, 88, 91, 92, 96, 111,
    112, 123–25, 134 (*see* also gift-
    blessings; also practice area)
refinement 25, 29–31, 60, 61, 63, 65,
    67, 76, 81, 83, 85, 86, 102, 136–42
    (*see* also energy: purification)
restrictions 25, 30, 59, 60, 63, 67, 73, 1
    79, 80, 96, 178
sensitivity 17, 62, 66, 90, 95, 100
solar (energy) 61, 92–95, 112, 113, 115
    (*see* also energy: channel(s); also
    solar (sun); also under time(s))
subtle types
    most subtle (root energetic) 30, 31,
        58–61, 80, 85–87, 176, 177, 180,
        181, 184
    subtle (emotional) 29, 31, 58–62,
        64–66, 75, 76, 79–81, 87, 91, 94,
        95, 99–102, 111, 123–31, 180
    very subtle (mental) 29, 58–61, 76,
        80, 82, 83, 100, 102, 113, 136,
        139, 141, 159, 162, 169, 180, 181
entanglement 8, 12, 14, 23–26, 36, 45–47,
    51, 57, 65, 86, 178, *see* also
    habitual tendencies
essential nature vi, vii, ix, 8, 14, 18, 19,
    22–26, 30, 34, 41, 47, 68, 70, 144, 177,
    182, 184
exercise, *see* movement practices
experience, *see* direct experience;
    phenomena
extraordinary awareness, *see* also
    realization; under awareness

F

faith ix, 18, 19, 24, 73, 132

fall, the 11, 18, 21, 23, 24, 28, 37, 38, 47, 53, 68, 88, 144, 146, *see* also perception: dual
fear 6, 10, 14, 30, 40, 47, 51, 55, 59, 63, 66, 70, 71, 86, 90, 145, 146, 170
fetter, *see* entanglement
field, *see* emptiness
fire energy center (navel), *see* under elemental energy, types
focus, *see* single-pointed focus
fourth estate, *see* realization
full meditative posture, *see* posture(s): seated
full-realization, *see* realization; stream

G
gazing 82–85, 89, 101, 102, *see* also vision(s)
gift-blessings 3, 24, 90, 92, 95, 132–35, 170
good and evil, *see* perception: dual
governing forces, *see* intelligences
grace 17, 25, 133
granthis, *see* under energy: restrictions

H
habitual tendencies vii, 6–8, 12–14, 21–23, 31, 45, 52, 53, 62, 65, 68, 72, 76, 82, 83, 86, 87, 115, 145–48, *see* also entanglement
half meditative posture, *see* posture(s): seated
health, *see* well-being
heart 21, 37, 40, 60–62, 69, 76, 79, 81, 83–85, 132, 135, 146–48, 156–61, 180, *see* also heart-mind
heart-mind 37, 61, 81, 83, 143–48, 159, 166–68, 173–75

I
ida, *see* energy: lunar; under energy: channel(s)
identity-body (ego, self) v, vi, ix, 6, 7, 9, 11–14, 16–29, 31, 34–40, 43–60, 62–66, 69, 70, 73, 75, 79, 80, 88, 101, 113, 115, 125, 143–47, 177, 178
imagery, *see* vision(s)
in-between 82–84, 148
indicators, *see* under path
inner heat, *see* bliss-warmth

insight 8, 29, 31, 32, 64, 65, 68, 84, 88, 91, 99, 101, 180, 181, *see* also awareness: awakened; also intention; also union
intellect 8, 12, 16–22, 36, 51, 56, 57, 60, 62–64, 78, 81, 113, 184, *see* also aggregates
intelligence, *see* aggregates; intellect; intelligent governing forces
intelligent governing forces 3, 16, 58–67, 85, 90–95, 132–35, 170
intention v, vi, viii, ix, 11–15, 52, 60, 61, 68, 73, 90, 91, 101, 132–35, 165, 173, 180–83, 185, *see* also insight
intuition 3, 40, 64, 66, 113, *see* also insight; also wisdom
investigation v, viii, 8, 18–20, 30, 31, 41, 42, 54, 57, 63, 65, 75, 76, 78, 79, 97, 99, 100, 112, 120–22, 128–29, 136–42, 181, *see* also single-pointed focus

K
karma 76, *see* also cause; also habitual tendencies
kundalini energy, *see* bliss-warmth

L
liberation 3, 14, 30, 51, 54, 69, 183
Light 29, 37, 39, 42, 44, 61, 62, 68, 69, 72, 80, 123, 185, *see* also All; also energy; also phenomena
loosening, *see* adjustment, meditative
lucid dreaming, *see* under sleep: states
Luminous Eye of Wisdom, Volume II 3, 57, 58, 61, 94, 102, 113, 114
lunar (moon) 92, 93, 95, 112 172, *see* also under energy; also under energy: channel(s); also under time(s)
phases 92, 93, 95

M
meditative posture, *see* posture(s)
memory, *see* aggregates
mental aggregates, *see* aggregates
meridian, *see* energy: channel(s)
method, stages overview, *see* under path
mind vii, 17–19, 21, 24, 27, 30–32, 36, 37, 61–63, 65, 69–71, 73, 74, 76, 77, 79, 81–86, 88, 97, 99, 100, 111, 113, 135, 143, 145, 146, 178, 180, 184, *see*

also awareness; also cognition; also
  heart-mind; also mindstream
mindstream 24, 29, 36, 51, 62, 73, 77,
  111, 120, 143, see also phenomena
moon, see energy: lunar; lunar
movement practices (various) 96, 97, 99
movement principle, see heart
mudras 101, see also posture(s)
mystic vision 7, 59, 61, 81–89, 101,
  104–10, 164–67, 170, 172–75, see also
  posture(s); also vision(s): secret
mystical union, see union
mysticism, see under path

N

nonconceptual, see emptiness; perception

O

object (of focus or investigation),
  see anchor; perception
ocean breathing, see under breath
offerings, see gift-blessings
One Unique and Unified, see All
ordinary awareness, see under awareness

P

padmasana, see posture(s): seated
path v, vi, vii, ix, 3–10, 13–15, 18–34, 38,
  43, 47, 54, 57, 73, 74, 95, 96, 111, 176,
  179, 180–82, see also realization
  assistance (getting help) viii, ix, 1, 6–8,
    10, 85, 88, 102, 114, 117, 119,
    132–35, 170, 176, 179–81
  authentic viii, ix, 3, 5, 8, 18, 20, 23–33,
    43, 46, 65, 74, 185
  benefits vi, viii, ix, 11–15, 17, 18, 37,
    100–102, 132, 180–85
  cautions, general 3–22, 65, 71, 78, 81,
    88, 146, 181, 182
  indicators 6, 7, 9, 10, 22, 32, 37, 60, 61,
    65, 66, 83, 86, 88, 113, 169, 179
    (see also vision(s))
  method overview 3–5, 27, 29, 30
  misconceptions vi, ix, 13, 14–24, 43,
    63, 82, 88, 90, 181
  mysticism v, vii, viii, 3, 6–8, 11, 13,
    18–20, 30, 32, 33, 36, 37, 44, 54, 66,
    90–94, 132–35, 184, 185
  teacher v, vi, viii, ix, x, 6–8, 10, 85, 88,
    98, 114, 132, 176, 180, 181, 184–85

theory, chapter descriptions 4–5
perception
  dual 7, 17, 19, 20–29, 31, 32, 34,
    36–38, 42, 43, 45–47, 59, 68, 78, 79,
    92
  field of perceiving (see emptiness)
  perceiver, perceived, perceiving
    (trinity) (see trinity)
personality, see identity-body
phenomena 8, 11, 15, 18, 19, 24–29, 31,
  32, 35, 36, 38, 39–47, 49–50, 53–55,
  59, 63, 65, 67–77, 79, 82, 85, 86, 88,
  90, 101, 112, 143–48, 159, 176–79,
  see also Light
pingala, see energy: lunar; under
  energy: channel(s)
posture(s) 98–102
  mystic vision 82–85, 104–10, 164–68,
    172–75
  seated 98–110
  sleep 104
practice area 3, 90–95, 132–35
prayer, see gift-blessings; intention
primordial awareness, see essential nature
progress, see path: indicators
projection 66, 87, 104, 169–71
psychic abilities, see intuition
purification, see energy: purification

R

realization v, vi, vii, xiii, xv, 3, 4, 7–9, 11,
  13–16, 18–21, 23–34, 37, 38, 40, 43,
  46–48, 52, 55, 57, 59, 60, 65, 68, 74,
  78, 79–82, 84, 86, 88, 176, 179–85,
  see also path; also union
realms viii, 3, 16, 17, 28, 52, 66, 86, 90,
  92, 181
rebirth, cycle of 3, 14, 15, 23, 32, 37, 41,
  47, 55, 71, 73, 86, 177
resistance breathing, see under breath
restrictions, see under energy
right view, see view
ritual, see gift-blessings; practice area

S

samadhi, see direct experience
self, see identity-body
self-realization, see realization
sense-desire, see identity-body
Shakti 37, see also emptiness; also heart

shakti energy, *see* bliss-warmth; energy
Shiva 37, 44, *see* also awareness;
   also mind
shushumna, *see* under energy: channel(s)
signs, *see* path: indicators;
   vision(s): secret
single-pointed focus 75–77, 113
sleep 7, 29–31, 55, 62, 68, 69, 83, 86–88,
   94, 96, 97, 102, 104, 111, 114, 176–79,
   see also well-being
   states (*see* also projection)
      deep 7, 29–31, 69, 83, 86–88, 104,
        176–79
      dream 7, 30, 31, 69, 70, 77, 82, 83,
        86–88, 104, 169–71, 176–79
solar (sun) 42, 68, 72, 92–93, 112, 164,
   177, *see* also under energy: channels;
   also under time(s); under energy
source vi, 18, 19, 21–23, 29, 35, 39, 40,
   42, 47, 53, 80, 185, *see* also All;
   also cause; also emptiness; also Light
space energy center (akash, throat),
   see under elemental energy, types
stillness principle, *see* mind
straying, *see* adjustment, meditative
stream, *see* bliss-clarity; realization; union
stream-realization, *see* realization
subtle energy, *see* under energy
suffering ix, x, 8, 11, 12–14, 17, 18, 20,
   21, 23, 24, 26–27, 37, 41, 45, 47,
   49–51, 53–55, 68, 70–72, 76, 86, 88,
   144, 183

T

teacher, *see* under path
theory, chapter descriptions 4–5
thought-stream, *see* identity-body
Tibetan rites, *see* movement practices
tightening, *see* adjustment, meditative
time(s) 32, 74, 92–94, 97, 182, 183
   cycle(s) 3, 62, 94, 95, 112, 170
   (*see* also rebirth, cycle of)
   lunar 92–95, 112, 113, 133, 170
   solar 92–95, 112, 113
tree of life ix, 12, 18, 21, 31, 82, *see*
   also union
trinity (three) 18, 32, 44, 53, 61, 79, 82,
   93, 111, *see* also bliss-clarity
tummo, *see* bliss-warmth; energy
turiya, *see* realization

U

unification, *see* union
union vii, 7, 8, 14, 19, 26–32, 37–39, 43,
   44, 47, 55, 58, 60, 61, 65, 72, 74,
   78–84, 176–85, *see* also bliss-clarity;
   also realization

V

vajrasana, *see* posture(s): seated
view 17, 25, 31, 38, 67–77, 81–85, 88,
   119, 143–48, 176–85, *see*
   also perception
vision(s), *see* also gazing
   inner (hypnogogic) 39, 82
   outer (external) 39, 82
   secret (mystical) 7, 31, 39, 59, 61,
      81–88, 101, 102, 104, 146, 156, 159,
      164–70, 172–75, 177
vitality, *see* elemental energy; well-being

W

water energy center (sacral), *see*
   under elemental energy, types
well-being 25, 51, 60, 96, 97, 99, 111
will 77, 88, 101, *see* also emptiness
winds, *see* elemental energy
wisdom vi, 9, 14, 20, 32, 34, 36, 47, 52,
   78, 81, 82, 86, 91

Y

yoga, *see* movement practices; posture(s);
union; well-being

About the Author

Raziyahu began his spiritual practice before age 7 and has taught mysticism for over 15 years. He was guided in formal meditative discipline for more than 8 years under his first teacher, and his orthodox Jewish and orthodox Catholic grandparents inspired his strong spiritual values and heartfelt devotion. After ministering later in life, Raz made the decision to set aside a 35-year martial arts career and turn his full attention toward advanced mystical practice. While hidden away in the California desert on a 6-month solitary retreat, he refined and deepened his mystical experiences and sealed realization. Many of Raz's veteran students, having received individual instructions, empowerments, and transmissions from him after his breakthrough, now aspire to teach and share the method as they draw nearer to their own realization.